The Southern Mystique

THE SOUTHERN MYSTIQUE

Howard Zinn

South End Press

CAMBRIDGE, MASSACHUSETTS

The "Introduction" appeared originally in slightly different form as "The Southern Mystique" in *The American Scholar*.

Part One includes a portion first published in slightly different form as "A Case of Quiet Social Change" in *The Crisis,* and brief passages from "A Fate Worse than Integration" were first published in *Harper's Magazine.*

Part Two includes a portion first published as "Finishing School for Pickets" in *The Nation*.

Part Three is an adaptation of "Albany: A Study in National Responsibility," first published as a pamphlet by the Southern Regional Council.

Cover design by Kyle G. Hunter
Front cover photograph (taken at a demonstration in Boston) by Lee
Lockwood
Back cover photograph by Jeff Zinn

Library of Congress Cataloging-in-Publication Data

Zinn, Howard, 1922–
    The Southern mystique / Howard Zinn.
        p. cm. — (The radical 60s ; v. 2)
    Originally published: New York : Alfred A. Knopf, 1964.
    Includes bibliographical references.
    ISBN 0-89608-680-1 (pbk. : alk. paper)
        1. Southern States—Race relations. 2. United States—Race relations.
    3. African Americans—Social conditions—To 1964. 4. African
    Americans—Southern States—Social conditions. 5. Southern States—
    Social conditions—1945– 6. United States—Social conditions—1945–
    I. Title. II. Radical sixties ; v. 2.

E185.61 .Z5 2002
305.896'073075'09046—dc21

                                                    2002029152

South End Press
7 Bookline Street, #1
Cambridge, MA 02139-4146
www.southendpress.org

06 05 04 03 02   1 2 3 4 5

To Fannie Lou Hamer

Contents

Preface to the South End Press Edition   ix

Acknowledgments   xi

Introduction   3

PART ONE
Is the Southern White Unfathomable?   15

PART TWO
The "Mysterious" Negro   87

PART THREE
Albany, Georgia: Ghost in the Cage   145

PART FOUR
The South as a Mirror   215

Preface to the South End Press Edition

Teaching and living in Atlanta, Georgia, in the black community of Spelman College and its environs, observing the growing
resistance to racial segregation in the city, I began to write about
what I saw. My first published article, in *Harper's Magazine,* reflected my thoughts about the possibilities for change in what
had seemed a society impenetrable and intransigent. When I
traveled to Albany, Georgia, to write a report on the mass
demonstrations of the black population in that city, I was forced
to reflect further on the nature of the American South. As a
white person close to black people in my college and in the
movement, I felt that I was in a special position to reflect on
white–black relations and their future. I began to reject the notion of a South totally different from the rest of the nation, and
this book was an attempt to argue that thesis.

The Southern Mystique

Introduction

PERHAPS the most striking development in the South is not that the process of desegregation is under way but that the mystique with which Americans have always surrounded the South is beginning to vanish.

I was as immersed in this mystique as anyone else as I drove into Atlanta for the first time on a hot August night seven years ago. It was raining, and my wife and two small children awoke to watch the shimmering wet lights on Ponce de Leon Avenue. For the last full day of driving, the talk and the look of people were different. The trees and fields seemed different. The air itself smelled different. This was the mysterious and terrible South, the Deep South, soaked in blood and history, of which William Faulkner wrote—and Margaret Mitchell and Wilbur J. Cash. White Atlanta had been ravaged and still knew it. Negroes had been slaves and still remembered it. Northerners were strangers, no matter how long they stayed, and would never forget it.

There was something about Atlanta, about Georgia, the Carolinas, that marked them off, as with a giant cleaver, from the rest of the nation: the sun was hotter, the soil was redder, the people blacker and whiter, the air sweeter, heavier. But beyond the physical, beyond the strange look and smell of this country, was something more that went back to cotton and slavery, stretching into history as far as anyone could remember—an invisible mist over the entire Deep South, distorting justice, blurring perspective, and, most of all, indissoluble by reason.

It is seven years later. I have lived these years inside what is often thought to be the womb of the South's mystery: the Negro community of the Deep South. My time has been spent mostly with the warm and lovely girls in my classes at Spelman; but also with the earnest young men across the street at Morehouse, with the strangely mixed faculties of the Negro colleges (the white and the dark, the silent and the angry, the conservative and the radical), with the black bourgeoisie of college presidents and business executives, with the poor Negro families in frame houses across the street and their children playing with ours on the campus grass. From this, I have been able to wander out into the glare of the white South or to cross into those tiny circles of shadow, out of sight, where people of several colors meet and touch as human beings, inside the tranquil eye of the hurricane.

The Southern mystique hovered nearby even on yellow spring afternoons when we talked quietly to one another in the classroom. At times it grew suddenly dense, fierce, asphyxiating. My students and I were ordered out of the gallery of the Georgia General Assembly, the Speaker of the House shouting hoarsely at us. One nightmarish winter evening, I was arrested and put behind bars. Hundreds of us marched one day toward the State Capitol where helmeted soldiers with rifles and gas masks waited. A dozen of us "sat-in" at a department store cafeteria, silent as the manager dimmed the lights, closed the counter, and ordered chairs piled on top of tables all around. I drove four hours south to the Black Belt country of Albany, Georgia, to call through a barbed wire fence surrounding the County Jail to a student of mine who was invisible beyond a wire mesh window. It was in Albany also that I sat in the office of the Sheriff of Dougherty County who a month before had given a bloody beating with a cane to a young Negro lawyer. And nowhere was the mystique so real, so enveloping, as on a dirt road in the dusk, deep in the cotton and peanut land of Lee County, Georgia, where justice and reason had never been, and where the night before bullets had ripped into a farmhouse belonging to Negro farmer James Mays and exploded around the heads of sleeping children.

And yet, I can say now after living intensely in the Deep South in exactly those seven years when the South itself has lived most intensely, that the mystique is dissolving, for me, and for others. The South is still the most terrible place in America. Because it is, it is filled with heroes. The South is monstrous and marvelous at the same time. Every cliché ever uttered about the South, every stereotype attached to its people, white and Negro, is true; a thousand other characteristics, complex and subtle, are also true. The South has not lost its fascination. But it is no longer mysterious. And I want to explain this by talking about those two groups who have been at the center of this mystery, the whites and the Negroes of the Deep South.

Although the darkness of the Negro physically suggests mystery, it is the white Southerner, oddly enough, who has been presented as the great national enigma. This, despite the whiteness of his skin, against which flaws and blemishes show up more easily, a whiteness unsullied by that admixture of Slavic and Latin blood found in the North, and kept homogeneous by the simple expedient of tossing over the wall in the night all offspring from black-white sexual encounter. The mystery of the white Southerner comes from a trait that he is presumed to possess in quantity and quality sharply distinct from that of everyone else. That trait is race prejudice.

Other white people, it is acknowledged, are color-biased. There is considered to be, however, something special about the quality of the white Southerner's prejudice. The Yankee is rather businesslike in his matter-of-fact exclusion of the Negro from certain spheres of ordinary living. The British imperialist was haughty and sure of himself. But the violence, the passion, the murderous quality of the white Southerner's feeling against the Negro has become a canon of American thought that is deep in our consciousness and our literature (and in European literature as well: Sartre's *La Putain respectueuse*). And what is more significant, although the outward signs of this prejudice are clear enough, at its core, at the *why* of this crazy feeling, is a mystery.

When reporter John Bartlow Martin wrote *The Deep South Says "Never"* right after the Supreme Court school-desegregation decision, he implied in the book's title itself that there was some ineradicable mystical hatred, so deep and so invisible in the white Southerner, that no blasts of social change could touch it. After I had lived a year or so in the Deep South, talking to and living next door to the same white people described by the author of that book, I began to suspect he was wrong. Six years later, I knew he was. Prejudice, discrimination, race hatred are real problems, to the point of viciousness, even murder. But their mystery, for those who will look hard, is gone.

I will not tangle with *cause*, because once you acknowledge *cause* as the core of a problem, you have built something into it that not only baffles people, but, worse, immobilizes them. Causation is not merely complex—it may be a problem impossible of solution, according to some of the new philosophers. Perhaps it is one of those metaphysical conundrums created by our own disposition to set verbal obstacles between ourselves and reality. Why not ignore cause as a general philosophical problem and concentrate on *result?* The point is devilishly, irreverently simple: if you can get a desired result, the mystery is gone. Stop fumbling with the *cause* of prejudice except for those aspects on which we can operate. A physicist may still not know what *really* is behind the transformation of matter into energy, but if he has figured out how to release this energy, his achievement is stupendous.

Atlanta is in the Deep South. Atlanta has as many crackpots, KKK sympathizers, country wool-hats, white supremacists, barbershop lynchers, vicious policemen as any Southern city. If the Deep South said "Never," Atlanta, too, said "Never." In 1958 it was tightly segregated. By 1963: the buses had desegregated; so had the public libraries, the rail and bus terminals, a number of theaters and restaurants downtown, the department store cafeterias, the opera, the municipal auditorium, the legitimate theater, the public schools, the colleges (public and private), several hotels, the plainclothes squad of the Police Department, the Fire Department, the baseball team, the tennis courts, the parks, the golf courses, the public swimming pools, the Chamber of Commerce, several professional organizations, the county committee of the Democratic Party, and even the Senate of the Georgia General Assembly!

These are all tokens, in relation to the total need, but they suggest what is possible. And now that they are won, obvious explanations can be advanced with great casualness: a flexible city administration, a layer of Negro intellectuals, a determined student movement willing to engage in civil disobedience, a band of white liberals who give a cosmopolitan salting to the country-style Talmadge ham. But none of this takes account of the fact that all the above forces are a minority of the population; that most of Atlanta's population, the overwhelming majority of its 350,000 white people, still consider Negroes inferior and prefer a segregated society; and that all these people could have prevented most of the change—by riot, by election, by boycott —*if they had cared enough*. They stood by passively and accepted, with the puniest resistance, a series of important changes in the sociolegal structure of the city.

There is, then, a key to the traditionally mysterious vault of prejudice locked inside the mind of the white Southerner. He cares, but *not enough*. Or, to put it another way, although he cares about segregation, there are things he cares about *more*. The white Southerner has a hierarchy of desires, in which many other things are rated higher than segregation: monetary profit, political power, staying out of jail, the approval of one's immediate peers, conforming to the dominant decision of the community. Desegregation came in varying degrees, to Atlanta and a hundred other places in the Deep South, in the face of persistent anti-Negro feelings in the community, simply because one or another of these desires, which stand higher in the Southerner's value-scheme, was threatened and the white Southerner chose to surrender.

Except as an academic exercise, there is no need then to probe the fog that inescapably shrouds the philosophical question of causation in race prejudice. What needs to be done is to decide for each group of whites in the community which value is more important and to plan a web of multiple tactics—negotiation, boycott, lawsuit, voting, demonstration—that will effectively invoke these priorities. In a rough semiconscious way, the actions of the federal courts and of Negro leaders in the South have aimed at this; a more deliberate use of the hierarchy-of-value concept would bring even more dramatic results.

The white man in the South is subject to the same simplicities and the same complexities that surround the human species of any color any place; he has certain biological needs, which he will try to satisfy whichever way he can; on top of this he has certain wants which he has learned from his culture—and because these often conflict with one another he has an unconscious set of priorities that enables him to make choices. He is subject to economic pressure and ambition. Also, if Jungian theory is correct and the notions of modern role psychology are valid (and I believe they are), he needs approval from certain people around him and seeks to play out the role society has cast him in. Beyond all this, as beyond all the frontiers of human knowledge, there is mystery in the behavior of the human animal. But it's time to clear from our minds that artificial and special mystique, so firmly attached to the Southern white, that has too long served as a rationale for pessimism and inaction.

But what of the black man—or woman? There is a strange and damnable unanimity among segregationists, white liberals, and Negroes on one fervent belief— the mystery of *négritude*—the irreducible kernel, after all sociological peelings, of race difference. The segregationist (White Citizen or Black Muslim) shouts this in all directions. The white liberal is subtle, sophisticated, and ingenious in the various ways he can express this: he sweetens it with sympathy or admiration or affection, he delights in the sheer thrill of a mystery. He cherishes it as a secret shared with his fellow liberals: "Yes, yes—we can never know what it is to be a Negro. No, no—they will never trust a white man, and we can't blame them." The Negro, robbed of other protection, clings to it, plays with it, turns it to his advantage when he can. Even the most perceptive of his literary leaders (James Baldwin, Ralph Ellison) use it with cunning, or with pride. And all of them, white liberal and Negro intellectual, fondle it and nurture it as men, having subdued a forest fire, might play with the last flames, too fascinated even in the midst of peril to put them out for good.

Physical difference is so gross a stimulus to human beings, cursed as they are by the gift of vision, that once it is latched onto as an explanation for differences in personality, intelligence, demeanor, it is terribly difficult to put aside. It becomes an easy substitute for the immensely difficult job of explaining personal and social behavior. Conservatives use it openly; liberals secretly, even unknowingly. It seems to be the hardest thing in the world to convince ourselves that once we've noted skin color, facial features, and hair texture, we have exhausted the subject of race—that everything beyond that is in our heads, put there by others and kept there by ourselves, and that all the brutal material consequences of centuries, from lynching to patronizing friendship, were spun from an original thread of falsehood.

The most vicious thing about segregation—more deadly than its immediate denial of certain goods and services—is its perpetuation of the mystery of racial difference. For there is a magical and omnipotent dispeller of the mystery; it is *contact*. Contact—but it must be massive, unlike those "integrated" situations in the North, and it must be equal, thus excluding maid-lady relationships of the South—destroys the man-made link between physical difference and behavior. Race consciousness is hollow, its formidable-looking exterior is membrane-thin and is worn away by simple acts of touch, the touching of human beings in contact that is massive, equal, and prolonged. The brightness of the physical-difference impression is relative; it stands out in that darkness created by segregated living, and it is quickly lost in the galaxy of sense impressions that come from being with a person day-in, day-out.

In our country, the kind of contact that rubs away race consciousness is possible only in rare places, and at rare times. But it exists, in scattered pockets of resistance to the norm. One of them is the Negro college, where white people can become so immersed in a Negro environment that they are oblivious, at least temporarily, of race. The fact that they live on an island, against which waves of prejudice roll from time to time, means that they slide back and forth from overconsciousness on some days to a blissful racial amnesia on others.

A white student, after she had spent several months living, eating, studying, playing in a totally Negro college environment, visited a nearby white college and returned saying: "How pallid they all seemed—all those white faces and sharp noses!" This is a startling example of race consciousness in reverse, but it is encouraging to see how quickly one can change the temper of racial awareness by an inundation of sense experiences.

Once the superficiality of the physical is penetrated and seen for what it is, the puzzle of race loses itself in whatever puzzle there is to human behavior in general. Once you begin to look in human clashes for explanations other than racial ones, they suddenly become visible, and even where they remain out of sight, it is comforting to know that these nonracial explanations exist. Disease began to lose its eeriness with the discovery of bacteria, although the specific problem of identifying each bacterial group remained.

So long as evil exists—and it exists in poisonous heaps, South and North—the raw material for mystery will be here. We can make the most—if we want to— of white mobs in Oxford, mass Negro indignation in Albany, blazing churches in Birmingham, gunfire on rural porches, and the sheer wonder of blackness and whiteness. But the specialness of the Southern mystique vanishes when one sees that whites and Negroes behave only like human beings, that the South is but a distorted mirror image of the North, and that we are powerful enough today, and free enough, to retain only as much of the past as we want. We are all magicians. We created the mystery of the South, and we can dissolve it.

PART ONE

Is the Southern White Unfathomable?

O N THE DAY following the federal court decision
that outlawed segregation on Atlanta buses, a Spelman
student named Anna Lois Clay (short, dark, a dancer)
described to me an incident of that morning. While she
was standing in a crowded bus headed downtown, she
saw a Negro man sitting near the front. A white
woman boarded the bus and, seeing an empty seat next
to the Negro man, said to him: "Will you please move
to the back so I can sit down?"

"No, ma'am," the man replied.

The woman grew agitated. "I'm asking you to move
back so I can sit down!"

The man shook his head. "I don't have to move back
any more, ma'am." He looked up at her and said quietly, "Don't you read the newspapers?"

Angry now, the woman called to the bus driver to
tell the man to move back. The bus driver shrugged his
shoulders. She insisted he call a policeman and at the
next stop he beckoned to one. The policeman boarded
the bus, listened to the woman, looked at the Negro and
the empty seat. He turned to the woman and said,

"Ma'am, don't you read the newspapers?" Then he stepped down from the bus.

In Atlanta and in other parts of the South, white people, without a revolution in the way they think, are undergoing a revolution in the way they act. This situation was not foreseen by the moderates who said the deep South would "never" change. It was not envisaged by the liberals who talked about the need for a transformation in the thinking process of the white Southerner before desegregation could be accomplished.

The liberals' assumption, that you must change the way people think before you change the way they behave, would be valid if every man were truly an island and if nothing but his own mental energy directed his actions. But man is beset by social pressures which often determine that his behavior will be contrary to the ideas he holds at that moment. (One example in reverse is that whites in the South assumed the Negro *liked* segregation because he adjusted his behavior to it.)

Thus, the "gradualist" in civil rights urges a slow process of changing people's minds by education to prepare the way for actual removal of segregation barriers. But we now have enough actual experience of social change in the South to say confidently that the opposite is true—that you *first* change the way people behave, by legal or extralegal pressures of various kinds, in order to transform that environment which is the ultimate determinant of the way they think.

But *can* you change the behavior of the white Southerner, in whom those mystic germs of prejudice have resided for centuries? And can you do it in such a way as to avoid creating in him the kind of violent resentments that may bring temporary compliance but later rebellion? There are several reasons for thinking it can be done.

For one thing, no longer does change depend on the *initiative* of the white person in the South. Nor does it depend on his approval. All it requires is quiescence. The Second Reconstruction now transforming the South has one feature strikingly different from the First: white people—liberal newspaper editors as well as the segregationist man in the street—are the followers of this movement rather than the leaders. What is called "intelligent white leadership" in the South is really the exercise of influence by some whites to get other whites to follow, however grumblingly, the leadership of Negroes. The initiative today is in the hands of militant Negroes, whose decisions on tactics are the parents of those decisions on law that are made in the courts and announced in the headlines.

Bus desegregation in Atlanta, for instance, embodied a sequence of events which has come to be rather standard. Several Negro leaders—motivated partly by idealistic dreams conceived in the bitter cavern of their own experiences, partly by the stirrings of Negroes elsewhere in the South—sat in front of the bus one day to create a legal test. The liberal newspapers of the city expressed regrets at the hastiness of the ministers. But the federal courts voided the local segregation laws. Then both the newspapers and city officials quietly urged compliance. Bus companies instructed drivers and began removing signs calling for segregation. Negroes began, slowly and in small numbers, to sit where they pleased on buses. Some whites reacted with stares or mutterings but most with indifference; there were no overt instances of violent protest.

Another explanation for recent nonviolent changes in white behavior is the heterogeneity of the white community. There is no such thing (and if common sense does not tell this, living in the South soon does) as a "typical" Southern white. Out of the same city of Macon in mid-Georgia come the Jewish segregationist lawyer Emanuel Bloch and the white Anglo-Saxon equalitarian newspaperwoman Margaret Long. In Augusta, there are racist Roy Harris and liberal ex-Governor Ellis Arnall. In one Atlanta barbershop I listened— prudently quiet since the barber was armed—to foul-mouthed rantings against "the niggers"; another time, in another barbershop a few blocks away, I noted the gentle approach to racial problems of a young barber who belongs to the Mormon church. One saleswoman in Rich's Department Store was hostile when she saw the address on my charge plate was "Spelman College"; another, seeing a Negro student and a white exchange student shopping together, and told they were attending the same classes, said, "That's nice, real nice."

True, the quality is varied, but—it might be argued —isn't it the *quantity* that counts? Is not the number of segregationists far greater than the others? Aren't there more Fascists than radical reformers, more pulpit bigots than preachers of the social gospel, more potential lynchers than potential heroes?

The answer—unsettling to our fond notions of democracy in America—is that the temper of a community, and its rules of conduct, are set by an élite of politicians, businessmen, newspaper owners, television station managers, top-drawer ministers, and bureaucrats in education. This embarrassing fact of rule from above can be utilized to speed social progress as well as to halt it. What distinguished the quiet school desegregation of Atlanta from the violent upheaval in Little Rock was not any measurable difference in the prejudice-count of the white populations, but the contrast in the quality of political leadership on city and state levels. Trembling Southern legislators who have stammered out their bewilderment in times when quick decisions were needed have been pitifully innocent of their own strength. The sociologists who postulate "power élites" are right for the most part, I think, but they often overestimate self-consciousness and confidence as characteristics of those élites.

Another feature of the Second Reconstruction—one that holds out real prospects this time for a permanent change in the Southern social structure—is that except in rare instances (Little Rock, Arkansas, and Oxford, Mississippi) change is not coming at the point of bayonets but through a mammoth, internal convulsion within the South itself. In almost all cases where desegregation has occurred, the white South has made its own decisions for acceptance. It made these decisions under pressure, and without enthusiasm, but it made them. It could have decided, if it wanted, to close down any school or terminal desegregated by law—and in almost all cases it chose not to. It could have decided to resist by force of arms, but did not. Department store owners could have kept lunch counters closed, but ultimately chose to open them integrated. Change has been swallowed hard and with much grimacing by the white South, but it has been swallowed. And once down, its potent contents will spread through the blood stream of the region.

Those who shook their heads sadly (the liberals) or

knowingly (the conservatives) in agreement with the prediction that the Deep South would not change for a long, long, long time, were analyzing the behavior of the Southern white in the narrow context of public opinion polls. These showed clearly, as they do now, that by far the majority of Southern whites favor a segregated society. The trouble with polls is that they wrench a situation from its life context and in doing so distort it. In life, people are not faced with clear-cut, yes-no decisions, but with a condition more like a multiple-choice test, in which no answer is exactly what the chooser wants. He must choose that which is closest to his desires, from a limited cluster of alternatives, in which every choice represents some degree of evil.

A few sociologists who specialize in race relations have known this for some time. When I first came to Atlanta, I sat in on a human relations group which was discussing how to desegregate the public library system, and I innocently suggested that we might convince city officials to do this by polling users of the library to prove that they would not object to the presence of Negroes. It is hard to say how such a poll would have turned out, but I was persuaded to withdraw the suggestion by Professor Mozell Hill, a sociologist then teaching at Atlanta University. Hill, to illustrate his point, told me of one city where the bus drivers had been polled in advance on their reactions to the hiring of Negro drivers. Many of them said they would quit their jobs if this were done. A few months later, several Negro drivers were hired. No one quit. It was not that the white drivers deliberately lied. They were probably really convinced that this is what they would do. But when they faced the actual—rather than the verbal

—choice of working along with Negroes or being without a job, they chose what to them was a lesser evil. I was soon to see this psychology in operation many times.

In the Deep South—the mystique surrounding white race prejudice notwithstanding—the white man can think of many things *worse* than desegregation, no matter how fervently, in a simple, no-risk poll, he declares his belief in the status quo. He may dislike to see a Negro sitting in the front of the bus, but if he is tired enough, and there is no other seat, he will sit down next to him. Most Southern white housewives, if the choice were a simple one, would not have their children go to school with Negro children; yet most would endure this rather than have no school at all for their children. A businessman will not bar Negroes from his lunchroom if by doing so he faces a prolonged and solid boycott that would cause his profits to drop.

Despite all the talk of resistance, the Southern white does not really want to sacrifice very much to keep his segregated society. The politician will not sacrifice political power, nor the businessman money, nor the professional man social approval. The ordinary citizen of the South does not want to go to jail to defend segregation. As Harry Golden has pointed out (in his famous scheme to put "Out of Order" signs on all "white" drinking fountains), the white Southerner is not happy about giving up a drink of water to preserve what a few have exaggerated as his "way of life."

The Southern white, in other words, has a hierarchy of values, in which some things are more important to him than others, and segregation, while desirable, does not mean as much to him as certain other values he has come to cherish. In this, he is simply behaving as all human beings do, selecting preferences, with the guidance of some subconscious order of priorities, in a field of limited possibilities.

The value-hierarchy idea was first suggested to me by an experience I had as an Air Force officer in World War II. When I was sailing to England on the *Queen Mary,* I and other air crewmen were given various duties on board ship. I was put in charge of the huge mess hall, where 16,000 men ate in four gigantic shifts twice a day. The last shift consisted of Negroes, since segregation was the rule, it will be recalled, for American armed forces in World War II. About the fourth day out, a mix-up in timing occurred and Negro troops poured down the gangways into the dining hall while many white soldiers were still eating. They streamed into the available empty seats and a white staff sergeant with a Southern accent called to me: "Lieutenant, will you ask this soldier to move from this table?"

I looked at the Negro sitting next to him. I was newly commissioned, filled with ideals about the war, and yet uncertain about how I should handle this. Finally I said, trying my best to assume the steadfastness of an officer pulling his rank: "You fellows are going overseas in the same war. Seems to me you shouldn't mind eating together. Sergeant, you'll have to sit there or just pass up this meal. I won't move either of you."

For a moment the man was silent. It was a long time to the next meal, and his face showed the inner battle between his immediate hunger and the long ancestry of his prejudice. Then he picked up his fork and finished his meal.

．　　．　　．

Our overly heavy sense of history has left us unpre-
pared for the possibilities of swift change in the white
South. We are too much impressed with the power of
the past—the social past of slavery, Civil War, Reconstruction; and with each individual's past—back to the
first cry of "nigger" in childhood. The nineteenth century became obsessed with history, and the twentieth
century with psychology; in both fields the weight of
heritage has been enormous because the resistance to
it has been so feeble.

There are enough examples at hand in the middle of
the twentieth century to indicate that the past need not
rest heavily on a determined people, but because most
of these examples are obnoxious to us (Hitler transforming the German people, the Communists burying
centuries in Russia and millenia in China) we hesitate
to affirm that today man has the power to move society
in *new* directions. The American preoccupation with
the Civil War has been crushing to suggestions for radical change; the Civil War Centennial, typically, has
become an excavation of old battle grounds rather than
a preparation for a new moral and political combat.
Transfixed by the past, we escape responsibility for
acting in the present. Thus history has become a burden
rather than a guide, as if it were a thousand-pound
compass strapped to our backs. Yet the changes in the
South, even of just these last five years, give evidence
that the past is elephantine only if we view ourselves
as pygmies.

As in the history of society as a whole, so in the history of individuals—the power of the immediate has
been overlooked. Nowhere is this oversight more cru-

cial than in the policies of our national leaders and
their local counterparts all over the country. Political
leaders, and those advising them, have never really
mined all the possibilities for purposive social change in
that old political adage which says that the public has a
poor memory. Or to put it another way, the public's
memory is a growing thing, and experiences both fresh
and powerful can push older recollections to the side.
The exciting thought for sociological consideration,
containing promise as well as risk, is that such experiences can be *created*.

Such a new dynamics of political leadership may
find suggestive material, I believe, in some of the work
of post-Freudian social psychology. There is also supporting evidence from recent historical studies of the
Reconstruction and post-Reconstruction eras. And then
there is the wealth of information, just waiting to be
pondered and applied, in the Southern experience of the
past few years. I would like to take a brief look at this
theoretical and historical data, before going on to explore some personal experiences in the South which tend
to support that theory, and add, if slightly, to that history.

Orthodox Freudianism, placing a heavy emphasis on
biological heritage and early childhood as determinants
of later behavior, made a revolutionary contribution to
scientific thought. But as with Newtonian physics and
Marxist economics, the tremendous act of creating a
new vocabulary led too many to believe that the last
word had been said. Persistent emphasis on the psychological heritage from the distant past made it difficult to see the immense possibilities for individual

change under the impact of immediate circumstance. With recent social psychological theory, we are getting closer, I believe, to an explanation of human behavior in the real world, as opposed to the world of the laboratory and the library.

Kurt Lewin, a refugee from Hitler who set up a Research Center for Group Dynamics in this country before his death in 1947, took from physics the concept of a "field theory." Instead of trying to abstract, from the distant past of an individual, an expected general behavior pattern, he concentrated on the entire field of influence acting on an individual in a real situation at a particular real moment. He wrote in *Field Theory in Social Science:* "According to field theory, behavior depends neither on the past nor on the future but on the present field." He did not ignore the influence of either past events or future expectations on the actions of individuals, but only rigorously excluded from consideration all influences except those operative *at the given moment.*

To show how a change in immediate circumstances could bring a change in habitual behavior, Lewin cited an experiment in which one girl, Sarah, with experience of aggressive behavior in a group dominated by autocratic leadership, began to spend time with another girl, Sue, from a group where co-operation and democratic leadership were stressed. Gradually, but dramatically, the behavior of each girl began to approximate that of the other, until by the ninth meeting they showed the same levels of autocracy-democracy in their actions.

By insisting that not only the *direction* of a pressure but also its *force*(which he measured and represented pictorially in *vectors*) was important, Lewin gave us a theoretical base for understanding the behavior of that white soldier I encountered on the *Queen Mary*. For the soldier, the power of several factors—his hunger, the authority of a "superior" in a military setting, the prospect of a long wait until the next meal—though operative only for one moment in time, could overcome for *that* moment all the years of prejudice-experience in his Southern past.

Lewin's work was continued by Dorwin Cartwright, who did laboratory experiments and field studies as part of the work in "group dynamics." In a 1951 article in *Human Relations,* Cartwright noted that the same kinds of people showed marked variations in behavior depending on what group they were in at the time. Aggressiveness and troublemaking changed dramatically depending on the "field" of human influence around at the moment, regardless of what had been noted as the "personality" of the individual whose behavior was being observed. Cartwright did not claim that a group setting was *totally* responsible for an individual's behavior, but "it is remarkable to what an extent a strong, cohesive group can control aspects of a member's behavior traditionally thought to be expressive of enduring personality traits." We can be more optimistic, field theory suggests, about change in Southern whites' behavior, if we begin to think about it not as the inevitable result of a fixed set of psychological traits, but as the response to a group atmosphere which is susceptible to manipulation.

The psychologist Harry Stack Sullivan, a contemporary of Lewin, also departed from Freud's stress on sex instinct and the libido. He believed that people behave the way they do mainly as a result of their interaction with other people, that they are not as bound by early experiences as the orthodox Freudians seem to believe. Sullivan posed the idea (derived from George Herbert Mead's notion of a "generalized other") of "significant others." Those "others" are people to whom a person consciously or unconsciously adjusts his behavior and whose power over that behavior is greater than the psychological heritage of infancy.

It was logical therefore that Sullivan should consider the psychoanalyst—who at the moment of contact with the patient was certainly one of the "significant others"—as not merely an observer but a "participant observer," who would not just passively study the patient, but have a deliberate effect on him. This is directly relevant to public policy in the area of race relations, for if both scholars and policy makers were to recognize that they themselves are "significant others," then their prescriptions could take into account the new situation created by their own participation. Specifically, for the South, a national government that foresees the results of its own activity as a "significant other" *affecting* white behavior might map much bolder policies than one that bases its moves on the passive situation represented by public opinion polls.

Freud's preoccupation with infantile sexual influences, with deep-rooted instinctual characteristics such as "the death wish," the "castration complex," the "totem" of father fixation, and the "taboo" of incest, led to a pervasive pessimism about man and society. It perpetuated the notion of fixity in human behavior, an idea to which men easily fall prey precisely because they live in a limited time-space capsule, in which the historical repetition of tragedy and despair suggests an inescapable "human nature."

Sullivan was more optimistic. He wrote in *The Interpersonal Theory of Psychiatry:*

> So far as I know, most of the ways in which one goes about being a human being could be very different from anything we have ever heard of. In other words, the human organism is so extraordinarily adaptive that not only could the most fantastic social rules and regulations be lived up to, if they were properly inculcated in the young, but they would seem very natural and proper ways of life.

Erich Fromm is another psychologist who stresses that what we have fondly, or despondently, thought of as "human nature" is to a large extent the result of a particular social setting. Fromm's distinction between "existential" facts which we can't escape, like birth, death, and the limitations of our life-span, and "historical" facts which are the result of circumstance, and which can be overcome, is pertinent. Prejudiced thinking and discriminatory behavior are "historical" facts which depend on a given situation and are not indissolubly linked to our biological heritage.

Herbert Marcuse's eloquent critique of the "neo-Freudians," particularly Fromm, in his *Eros and Civilization* is actually an affirmation of the idea that one must change society; but because he believes strongly in the Freudian categories, he sees Fromm, Sullivan, and the others as underestimating the power of the present civilization vis-à-vis the individual. Marcuse thinks they are utopian in their expectations of what people

can do today. Stressing the power of forces like the
"death instinct," he argues that hope for the future "in-
volves a fundamental change in the instinctual as well
as cultural structure." This stress on "instinct" leads
necessarily to a greater pessimism. Leaving the larger
questions aside and focusing on the limited field of race
relations, I would say the evidence indicates that immediate environment rather than any instinctual hostility is the crucial determinant.

Closely allied to "field theory" is the idea of "situationism" which has been developed by a number of
American social psychologists, notably Gardner Murphy. In his book *Personality,* he writes:

> Situationism maintains simply that human beings
> respond as situations require them to respond, and
> that whatever their biological diversities, they will,
> if capable of learning, take on the attributes which
> the situations call for. . . . Given a changed sit-
> uation, there is a changed role and consequently a
> changed personality.

Murphy goes beyond Sullivan, who was still impressed by formative experiences in early childhood:
"For the situationist it is not the slow and arduous
process of fundamental character formation that is involved . . . it is rather the fulfillment, in the adult as
in the child, of the day-by-day requirements. . . . Indeed, a child may throw to the winds his entire previous
experience and react almost like a chameleon to his
new environment. . . . The present situation may be
far more important than any past experience."

Our overemphasis on physiological factors leads to
the self-fulfilling prophecy, Murphy points out. Over-

conscious as we are, for instance, of certain biological factors operating on adolescents and on the aged, we treat them accordingly. Their resultant behavior is then not natural but shaped by our participation. We have created a *role* for them by our expectations, and so they proceed to play that role. It seems we have hardly begun to explore the possibility of creating new roles in others by changing our own.

Stressing the *openness* of human behavior, Murphy writes that there is no one "real" attitude of a person:

> There are indeed many *potential* attitudes which are real, normal, human, and important, but none can appear and function except in a certain situation. . . . Since no two situations are ever alike, no personality is ever twice the same. Such continuity as there is arises largely from the relative continuity of the situations that the person confronts day in and day out. Personality could almost be defined as the integration of all the roles that a particular person has to enact.

This notion of "role-playing" is important in understanding the malleability of human behavior. We have always tended to confuse the role that a person was playing really to suit the expectations of "significant others" with what we thought was his basic, rooted personality. In connection with this, social psychologists speak of social reinforcement, where the continual reverberation between one's behavior and others' expectations leads to a behavior far more extreme than was justified by the initial stimulus. We might wonder then: how much of what prejudiced persons do is "reinforced" behavior, turned in one direction by an original pebble of experience? This behavior is not so solidly based in "personality" or "instinct" as we thought, and is therefore amenable to sweeping change.

Gordon Allport, author of *The Nature of Prejudice,* is a social psychologist who grapples more closely with specific problems in race relations. Allport's concept of "functional autonomy" leaves him less frightened by the power of the past. He wrote that "motives are contemporary" and are "not bound functionally to historical origins or to early goals, but to present goals only." Like the other psychologists we have mentioned, Allport's theory of behavior gives us a basis for more optimism in changing the way people act. With Lewin, Sullivan, Allport, man is more free than bound. This view can have a liberating influence on those who accept it, can give us both the confidence and the sense of responsibility we need to lead the communities of the South, as well as of the North, in the direction of desirable social change.

All of this new theory in social psychology seriously undermines the classic sociological view of William Graham Sumner that "stateways" cannot change "folkways." For some time now, observer-sociologists have been citing evidence from case studies or experiments to show how wrong Sumner's emphasis was. Arnold Rose, five years before the school desegregation decision of the Supreme Court, was arguing that the power of authority could revoke traditional discriminatory practice and bring about a new situation, with a minimum of trouble. He pointed to integration in the armed forces. He noted too the desegregation by edict of the Catholic schools in St. Louis in 1946 and 1947. At first there was some protest, but after six months the controversy settled down and it seemed as if the new pattern had been eternal.

One of the arguments against "forcing" a change through the exertion of authority is that it will leave a residue of hostility which will ultimately break out in disorder and perhaps even reverse the direction of events. I agree that such hostility would exist, behind the compliant behavior, in the new situation. But it seems to me that critics of authoritative change have failed to make an important distinction. Some changes, such as a change to segregation, bring about a situation which will remain indefinitely productive of hostility because of its essential conflict with a larger moral value and with the self-interest of the repressed group. Other kinds of changes produce a situation which is not only more in accord with widespread human values and interests, but which, in itself, will increasingly undermine the old belief. In other words, bringing white Southerners into contact on an equal basis with Negroes will ultimately break down that artificial suspicion which separation helped to foster, and the strain of the first encounter will disappear.

If United States national leadership had paid more attention to sociological investigations of recent years, it might have become aware of some clues to the possibilities for directed change. One such experiment tested the difference between the verbal attitudes and the actual behavior of customers who for the first time encountered Negro salespeople in a store. These customers, who had earlier expressed in words a strong prejudice against Negroes, went through the sales process, attended by a new Negro clerk, with no apparent difference in behavior. At that moment of test, they were faced with a conflict between the ingrained racial prejudice of their past and their immediate desire to get on with their shopping, to avoid having to go to another store or wait for another clerk. The immediate need won out. Operative here also was the element of conformity, the fact that the actual existence of Negro salespeople, as an apparently established fact, was a sign that *others* had already accepted it.

Perhaps the most dynamic union of recent social psychological theory and current desegregation practice has been made by Professor Thomas Pettigrew, a Harvard University sociologist. Pettigrew deplores "the relative neglect of situational variables in interracial behavior" and gives many examples to show that Southerners "seem fully capable of immediate behavioral change as situations change." In his article "Social Psychology and Desegregation Research" in the *American Psychologist,* written in 1961, Pettigrew stresses the element of conformity as a powerful determinant of Southern white behavior. He talks of "the latent liberal"—the white Southerner who really does not "feel" prejudice toward the Negro, but who *behaves* as if he does because of the situation around him. Such a person is on the edge of change, if only someone in authority can help create the right atmosphere. "Firm and forceful leadership," Pettigrew insists, is what makes the difference between peaceful integration and bitter resistance.

A historical explanation of racial problems turns from pathos to hope when Erich Fromm's "existential" facts of instinct, geography, race, infantile sexuality, and the collective unconscious, are set aside,

and we look closely at his "historical" facts of circumstance and situation. The "Sambo" personality which
Stanley Elkins so provocatively discussed in his book
Slavery—the beaten-down and submissive Negro, becomes explainable as the product of the plantation's
closed society. That personality also becomes, Elkins
suggests, reversible. And indeed, the proud Negro
demonstrator today appears by the thousands in exactly those little towns and hamlets of the Black Belt
that produced silence and compliance half a generation
ago.

The most forceful historical attack on the notion that
the South's racial mores constituted some unchangeable
"folkway" came with the publication of C. Vann Woodward's *The Strange Career of Jim Crow* in 1955.
Woodward was troubled by the common belief that segregation was an ineradicable fact of Southern life and
history. With the very first sentence of his book, he
seemed determined to destroy that idol. "The people of
the South," he began, "should be the last Americans to
expect indefinite continuity of their institutions and social arrangements."

Woodward went on patiently to cite the evidence.
The tight legal framework of segregation in the South, he
pointed out, far from being an immutable heritage from
the distant past, was of fairly recent construction. Slavery had no need for a rigid enforcement of segregation.
And although Radical Reconstruction measures after the
Civil War produced neither the equalitarian society imagined by romanticists of the period nor the black domination pointed to in traditionalist Southern mythology,
they did introduce the Negro to political power and did
give him equality in a few areas of Southern life. That

political participation, and those few elements of equal treatment, did not end abruptly with the Compromise of 1877 but continued for decades. Negroes continued to vote in large numbers until the turn of the century. For instance, in Louisiana, 130,000 Negroes were registered to vote as late as 1896. The number then fell to 1,300 in 1904.

The idea then that there was a long and persistent, therefore perhaps "natural," tradition of legal segregation in the South, broken briefly and unnaturally by the Reconstruction Acts and restored quickly in 1877, is simply untrue. The first Jim Crow law was not passed anywhere in the South until more than ten years after the end of the Reconstruction. Transportation and public facilities were open to Negroes in many places.

Woodward, after quoting Sumner's statement that "legislation cannot make mores," goes on to say: "Whether railways qualify as folkways or stateways, black man and white man once rode them. Later on, the stateways apparently changed the folkways—or at any rate the railways—for the partitions and Jim Crow cars became universal. And the new seating arrangement came to seem as normal, unchangeable and inevitable as the old ways."

The point of it all is that there is nothing indestructible, nothing frozen, nothing "natural," in the Southern pattern of race relations. If racial integration in some form could persist in the South, not only during the Radical Reconstruction period with its forced situation but for decades after that, then racial separation clearly is no mysterious necessity of Southern life but rather the product of historical circumstance. And man can change historical circumstance.

Beyond the evidence of social psychology and history, support for optimism about the white South is found also in the existential humanism of Jean Paul Sartre. He wants us to stop excusing evil by making it the responsibility of God, instinct, or some other determinant of the past. Man "is condemned at every instant to invent man"; that is, we all start in every situation from scratch and can make what we want of our lives. To say, as Sartre does, that there is no basic human nature, is to throw overboard the comforting notion that we are fundamentally designed to do good. But this concept also discards the debilitating idea that some basic evil in man's nature bars the creation of a good society.

The tragic flaw in the gradualist approach to racial discrimination is the assumption (an unconscious one) of *inaction* on the part of the observer. The assumption shows itself clearly in the reliance on poll-taking to test the possibilities for change. Poll-taking can *only* measure the past because the pollster is a neutral individual who introduces no directed force into the present field of influence of the person being polled. As soon as we turn from poll-taker into activist, we can change drastically the environment which surrounds the other person and can confront a long-standing but passive past with a just-born but vibrant present. Once we change our assumptions about ourselves and see ourselves as active molders of the situation, the old possibilities fall aside and new ones appear.

I have been discussing: changes in behavior coming before changes in belief; the role of leadership; the heterogeneity of the white Southern community; the hierarchy of values; the power of the immediate situation in determining how people act; the theorist as an active part of the social field. Now we need to see if we can find illustrations of these ideas in a small personal sampling from the events that sweep, every hour of every day now, across the South.

Two Spelman College girls—one from New Rochelle, New York, and the other from Newnan, Georgia—accompanied my wife, me, and our son on a motor trip from Atlanta to Asheville, North Carolina. At lunchtime, we found ourselves in Athens, Georgia, an antebellum plantation town where the Daughters of the Confederacy spirit reigns and where a year ago mobs rioted against the entrance of the first two Negroes into the state university. We parked and discussed what to do about lunch. (As John Howard Griffin has shown in *Black Like Me,* white people take for granted those fundamental conveniences, like places to eat and sleep, which Negroes on the road in the Deep South have to agonize over.) We could stop at a drive-in and bring food into the car; we could find a restaurant in the Negro part of town, where whites might be served; we could seek out the bus terminal, which legally, if not actually, was desegregated; we could try to get served at the Holiday Inn, where we had no legal right to be served under the present interpretation of the Fourteenth Amendment. Although we had the least chance of being served at the Holiday Inn, we decided to give it a try.

We entered the dining room, walked to a table, and sat down. The restaurant was half-full. A waitress saw us, turned, and disappeared behind swinging doors. We were quite sure she had gone for the manager, who would give us the usual courteous statement: "I'm sorry, but our rules don't permit us to serve colored people here. There's a nice restaurant on——Street where you folks could have something to eat." The waitress was gone for several minutes; we waited. Then she returned with menus and five glasses of water, her pencil poised to take our orders. The food tasted especially good to us. As I paid the check, I asked the manager, a young, pleasant-looking man: "Does serving us represent a policy of Holiday Inn now?" "No, our policy is segregation," he replied. "But once you were in and sitting down, I just didn't feel like asking you to leave."

One of the values which middle-class Southern whites cherish, even more than segregation, is freedom from embarrassment. At various times, Negroes in the South have been admitted to "White" places simply because they showed up unexpectedly; creating a scene would have been more embarrassing for the owner than simply accepting them quietly and rationalizing it as a one-time exception. Managers, administrators, and organization leaders infinitely prefer to settle these little problems by telephone or mail; there is something about a direct face-to-face rebuff to a Negro which is a little unsettling. A rejection in writing is easier on the conscience. And we should allow for some unmeasurable, fluctuating combination of conscience and self-interest in the behavior of human beings.

In face-to-face contacts, the decision has not always been in the Negro's favor, for the conflict in values involved is a close one. The decision-maker may find it preferable to go through the momentary embarrassment of turning the Negro away rather than have to explain later to others why a Negro was admitted. But we have seen again and again that there is a far better chance of acceptance if a direct confrontation occurs. A person with experience in race relations will never telephone in advance to *ask* if a place will admit Negroes, but will simply go ahead with an actual test.

The old-style conservative Negro avoided, and still avoids, such situations because he says he does not want to be "embarrassed." More militant Negroes— and their numbers are growing—use embarrassment as a weapon against segregation rather than as a bar to action. They start from the simple, reasonable assumption that the rejecting white has more cause to feel embarrassment than the rejected Negro. Even if a Negro is admitted in such a situation as a temporary expedient, this often heralds a permanent breakdown in the segregation pattern; every time the line is stepped on it becomes fainter. And even if the Negro who enters the situation in person is turned back, the act of confrontation and the discomfort of refusal (which *is* an inner feeling of many Southern whites, I am convinced) set up a psychological pressure which one day will have an effect.

Several years ago, in another part of the United States, some restaurants were polled on whether or not they would admit Orientals. The response was overwhelmingly negative. But when, weeks later, an actual Chinese couple showed up at these same restaurants, they were served in almost all cases. There is a social force generated by the flesh-and-blood presence of another human being which makes it incomparably more difficult to discriminate than one can in instances where a decision can be made in the seclusion of one's office.

It should be possible to analyze the value systems of

decisive persons and groups and to fit actions deliberately to these systems. In practice, what we find most
often is a pragmatically shifting series of maneuvers, a
search for openings, a flexible but insistent pressing
forward until a rampart sways and falls.

On the afternoon of May 22, 1959, Dr. Irene Dobbs
Jackson, a professor of French at Spelman College, accompanied by a young white faculty wife from Spelman, walked through the electrically operated door of
the marbled and modern Carnegie Library in downtown Atlanta, went to the front desk, and filled out a
membership application. She turned it in, and the slim
girl behind the desk handed her a new membership
card. The girl's voice was calm, but her hand trem-
bled slightly, perhaps because Dr. Jackson was the first
Negro ever to receive a membership card at a "white"
library in Atlanta.

At the same moment, on the second floor of the library, violinist and music professor Earl Sanders, a be-
spectacled, dark-skinned young man, whose outbursts
of good humor were a counterpoint to a powerful indignation, was thumbing through stacks of records to
find some chamber music he wanted. Exactly three
weeks before, while looking at records in the same
room, he had been asked to leave. Now, as he ap-
proached the check-out desk, the attractive girl sitting
there noted his selections with a friendly smile, and he
walked out.

The desegregation of the public library system in the
city of Atlanta took place quietly. Not until after the
fact did the newspapers announce to the community

that the main library and its fourteen branches, formerly reserved for whites, were now open to all. Atlanta Negroes, as word spread slowly among them, were surprised and gratified. There had been no lawsuit, no headlines, no violence. To explain the event, we need to examine a number of intertwining threads which knotted together in May of 1959, and which when unraveled, afford a glimpse into the subsurface mechanics of peaceful, purposeful social change.

A handful of Spelman students and faculty members, conscious of the unplanned and violent cataclysms that have shaken the world in this century, had been talking about the idea of deliberate social change. In a seminar on the philosophy of history, we explored two approaches which have dominated intellectual speculation: first, the notion that some great force, inscrutable like God, or ascertainable like economic necessity, is working behind the scenes of the human drama; and second, the more recent empiricist attempt to attack problems piecemeal by scientific scrutiny of individual phenomena rather than by insight into some universal explanation. We found ourselves critical of both these approaches, because they implied a passivity on the part of the intellectual, whose eye was at the telescope or the microscope but whose hands were rather idle.

More provocative than these ideas was one expressed by Charles Frankel in *The Case for Modern Man:* man is not a feeble creature pecking with a tackhammer at an impenetrable steel fence, but a free and mighty agent who, while studying the determinants of social change, can become a chief determinant himself. The potency of this idea actually has already affected some of the traditional schools of thought: the church fosters more and more activists for social reform; and the Marxists have shifted the emphasis from "inevitability" and the strength of "material forces" to the will and power of the Communist Party. Perhaps the atom-splitting of scientists has invested both communists and clerics with a new sense of command.

In our discussions at Spelman we played with the notion that man can coolly and deliberately locate a particular problem, survey the forces standing in the way of a solution, and either skillfully navigate around obstacles or, when the balance of power is just right, bowl them over. Translated into action and applied on a very modest scale, this kind of thinking played a part in the peaceful desegregation of the Atlanta public-library system, which opened to 150,000 Negroes of that city a wealth of books, paintings, and recorded music.

My students were at that time feeling uncomfortable about confining their studies to books while the South was being shaken by ideological and political upheaval. Why not select, out of the mass of events in the integration crisis, a limited field of combat where the enemy was weak and the possibility of gaining allies strong, and set out deliberately to occupy a tiny bit of territory? Why not plan and carry through to victory a minor skirmish in the big battle, through purposeful and rational action? The tactics, not quite customary for young women from a decorous and conservative Negro college, were to be those of guerilla warfare.

The library system was singled out for attention because it was a situation small enough to be handled by our little group, yet significant in its importance for the entire community. The relationship of forces seemed

favorable. Atlanta's city administration, which super-
vised the libraries, had been showing more flexibility
as it watched the growing Negro vote. The policy of
separate libraries was not written into law; it was simply an administrative rule of the library's Board of
Trustees, and it could be changed by action of the
Board, on which the Mayor was an important influence. At that time, various groups, particularly the
inter-racial American Veterans Committee, had tried to
get the Mayor to act.

Not the least of the factors we considered was that
action to desegregate the Atlanta library system represented a genuine need of students and faculty in the Atlanta University Center and of the city's Negro community. Of the three city libraries built especially for
Negroes, one was a newly erected showplace, part of
the post-war rash of attempts to introduce a bit more
equality into the "separate-but-equal" premise of Southern life. But the Carnegie Library had no match in the
Negro community. Built in downtown Atlanta some
thirty years before, it housed an impressive collection
of books in all categories, as well as paintings and re-
cordings, which were available for loan. The "for
whites only" label on the world's great literature was
not only a moral challenge but a practical obstacle to
learning.

As a first step, it was decided that students and Negro faculty, heretofore reluctant in the face of certain
rejection, should begin visiting the Carnegie Library
whenever they needed books unavailable elsewhere.
They expected to be rebuffed. But the visits would continue. So, the advance guard of a gradually increasing
stream of Negro visitors began passing through the

electric-eye entrance to the Carnegie Library. It was accidental irony that the first book sought in this campaign was John Locke's *An Essay Concerning Human Understanding*. The Spelman student who requested this was given the same treatment that subsequent Negro visitors were to receive: a courteous query as to whether the Negro branch had been tried, and then assurance that the book would be sent to the Negro branch and made available there. When a student said the book was needed immediately, she was told it could be studied right there in the library, in a special room downstairs, or in the office behind the main desk—anywhere, so long as there would be no contact with the white patrons.

Here was a typical Southern paradox: across the street from the library, in one of Atlanta's leading department stores, Negroes and whites could brush by each other at the counters, try on the same clothes, and, thanks to the irresistible impetus of the profit motive, be treated as near-equals. But nonsense has been uttered with aplomb for a long time in the South, and no one proved better at it than degree-encrusted library officials. Spelman and Morehouse College students visiting the Carnegie Library accepted whatever service was offered them, and left. Their purpose was simply to make the library aware that Negroes were in need of its facilities.

The Atlanta Council on Human Relations, meanwhile, had been working on the problem. This newly formed inter-racial group was headed by a white Unitarian minister, Edward Cahill, and the dynamic Whitney Young, then Dean of the Atlanta University School of Social Work. They began a sixteen-month campaign of persistent effort to convince the Library Board of Trustees, through detailed research and rational argument, that Atlanta libraries should be open to all. They collected statistics, made special maps, and referred the Library Director pointedly to the American Library Association's Bill of Rights, which says that "as a responsibility of Library service there should be no discrimination based on race or nationality." The Library Board remained unmoved, and the Council on Human Relations wearily announced this fact in February of 1959: "The Council urges all groups and individuals in the city to take such action as they deem appropriate to persuade the Library Board to desegregate the tax-supported facilities of the public library system."

With this, Spelman and Morehouse College students stepped up their visits to the Carnegie Library. In March, I paid a visit to the Director of the Atlanta library system, to probe the prospects for desegregation. He was discouraging. Of course, he assured me, the policy was not his desire, but a rule upheld by the Board which he was bound to enforce. No, he could not take the initiative in making a change. If Negroes began to use the library there would probably be violence. If this was his fear, I suggested, why not desegregate quietly, since there would otherwise be a lawsuit and the change would come anyway, with more publicity.

In the event of a court order to desegregate, the Director said matter-of-factly, he would close the libraries, as Governor Faubus had closed schools in Little Rock, to prevent violence. Surely, I said, white people who use your library would not riot over the use of the library by a few Negroes. You don't know these folks, he replied. The interview was over.

The library director's argument was the same one advanced so often in the South on the eve of change: there will be trouble. But in 90 per cent of the cases where desegregation had already taken place in the South (though one would never know this from reading newspaper headlines), there had been no violent reaction at all, only quiet if grudging acceptance. And although there is never any way of guaranteeing an absence of trouble, the probabilities in a case like this were on the side of peaceful change. We proceeded therefore to prepare a suit in federal court, and Whitney Young and I took the responsibility for getting plaintiffs, money, and legal help.

Just a few months earlier, the federal courts in Atlanta had given two favorable decisions, one desegregating the city's transit system, the other barring discrimination on grounds of race in the admissions policy of the University of Georgia. Several years before, a lawsuit had forced the municipal golf courses in Atlanta to admit Negroes. And in one Virginia county the mere threat of a lawsuit had opened up libraries to Negroes.

Our first job was to find plaintiffs, and this was not easy. A number of students were anxious to file suit, but they were discouraged by the complications of obtaining parental consent and of meeting other technical requirements, such as residence. Many Negroes were subject to economic reprisal if they dared participate in court action. I began to appreciate the work of the NAACP in handling lawsuits when I saw how difficult it was to get plaintiffs, something I had always assumed was no problem. But finally, two people came forward.

One was a young minister named Otis Moss, who was doing advanced study in theology and had often suffered from the inadequacy of the library facilities available to him. Moss's wife was a student in my American History course, articulate and intelligent. Moss himself, slim and very quiet, hardly seemed a social actionist. (I began to make out the depth of the man only a year later at a mass protest meeting in Atlanta when the apparently shy Reverend Moss lifted the crowd to a state of high emotion with a magnificent speech.)

The other plaintiff was Irene Dobbs Jackson, Professor of French at Spelman College, a friend and colleague, who said quietly as we sat having coffee in the Snack Shop on the campus, "It's what my husband would be doing if he were alive." Irene Jackson's rocklike strength had been put to its most severe test when her husband, a prominent Atlanta minister, died, leaving her with six growing children. She continued their education somehow, took four of them to France with her, where she studied for several years and received her doctorate at the University of Toulouse. Dr. Jackson came from a well-known Atlanta family. Her sister, Mattiwilda Dobbs, a Spelman College graduate, became famous because she was the first Negro to sing a starring role with the Metropolitan Opera Company. Her father, John Wesley Dobbs, was one of Atlanta's most distinguished citizens, a militant battler for equal rights and a great orator in the old Southern tradition. I heard him keep a crowd of thousands in an uproar one night at the Wheat Street Baptist Church. "My Mattiwilda was asked to sing here in Atlanta," he thundered at one point, "but she said, 'No sir! Not while my daddy has to sit in the balcony!' " Irene Dobbs Jackson told me: "Why, I've passed by the Carnegie Library a hundred times, and always wanted to go in. I think it's time."

Student visits to the Carnegie Library were now stepped up. City officials were apparently becoming uneasy, because a high municipal officeholder telephoned an Atlanta University administrator to plead that legal action be held up until the adjournment of the state legislature, which was in constant battle with the city administration.

What happened shortly after this, on May 19, 1959, I will quote from the notes I made on that day:

> Tuesday, May 10th: made an appointment to see Whitney Young at 2 P.M., to discuss with him next moves in suit to desegregate library system. Whitney told of an interesting development which might change things. A member of the Library Board had called him that morning, said he was disturbed at hearing that lawsuit was pending on library situation, wanted very much to avoid lawsuit. Whitney told him there was long history of conferences, requests, etc., and we were going ahead, and as a matter of fact had appointment at 2 P.M. with the parties involved in the suit to discuss pending action. The Board member said don't do anything, call me at 2 P.M. before talking to parties involved, and meanwhile will try to get lunch meeting of Board together.
>
> We talked a few minutes, then the Board member called. Library Board had just met at Atlanta Athletic Club. Whole Board was there. Mayor

was there. Chief of Police, City Attorney there.
Library Director was there. Decision was to change
policy. Mayor told the Board they had been foolish long enough. The Board member told Whitney hold off a few days, just long enough to allow
Director to inform staff of change.

Whitney and I agreed that we would give them
Wednesday and Thursday, test it out Friday and
for a week thereafter. Agreed I would go with
Mrs. Jackson to Carnegie Library Friday.

So it was that Friday, May 22, 1959, four of us rode
downtown to the Carnegie Library: Dr. Irene Jackson,
Professor Earl Sanders, myself, and Pat West, the
charming and spirited Alabama-born wife of a Spelman
philosophy professor. Irene Jackson joined the library,
and Earl Sanders took out his long-sought records. Later that week two Spelman students and one Morehouse
student walked into a "white" branch library on Peach-
tree Street and gave it its initiation.

As predicted by all groups who had asked integration, the desegregation decision caused no great com-
motion. Not until five days after the Board action did
the newspapers carry the story, and by then it was an
accomplished fact. The library director received a few
angry letters, Dr. Jackson was kept awake one night by
nasty telephone calls: "You that integratin' nigger?"
"This is the KKK." And as she sat at a library table
reading, that first day, a man came by and slammed his
books down hard on the table in voiceless protest. But
the general reaction was an enormous silence. One white
Atlantan said in a letter he sent to the *Atlanta Constitution* that he had lived in Atlanta all his life and never

knew the libraries were segregated, and he felt ashamed.

At a press conference a few days later, Georgia Governor Ernest Vandiver predicted that voluntary segregation would continue at the library because integration "does not represent the thinking or the wishes of the vast rank and file of colored citizens who would prefer to use their own library facilities." He turned out to be wrong, for the Carnegie Library, in the several years since it was integrated, has been used constantly by Negroes, without any trouble from whites. Mayor William Hartsfield turned out to be a better prophet than the Governor, when he told reporters: "A public library is a symbol of literacy, education, and cultural progress. It does not attract troublemakers."

In the library episode, a number of our hypotheses are underlined: Negroes acted, and whites reacted. The reaction of the whites was consistent with their particular value-schemes. The Mayor, dependent on Negro votes for election, saw a gain in popularity among Negroes which would not be offset by white disaffection, for the library was not, by its nature, an emotional issue; its users were not likely to be rabid on the race issue. Even if the library users were not delighted at the idea of Negroes using "their" library, they were not so unhappy as to cramp their own needs by staying away or by creating a scene in the genteel atmosphere of the reading room. The Library Board did not gain any political advantage by changing its policy; but it also would not have gained anything by battling with the Mayor, whose favor it wanted. And behind all this was the impending lawsuit, which would undoubtedly result in a court desegregation order, with attendant publicity. So the choice was not between segregation and

desegregation but between quiet and noisy desegregation. As for library employees, like most employees,
their supreme value was keeping their jobs; so, they
were likely to carry out policy as directed from above,
no matter what it was, and whatever their personal
wishes.

This analysis of the advantages that were weighed
does not take account of the element of genuine idealism present in the Mayor, in some Library Board members, in some library employees. But such idealism unfortunately is rarely preponderant enough to change a
situation where one value clearly outweighs another. It
can be important in circumstances where the advantages are so evenly balanced that even the feather-
weight of social conviction may tip the decision-making
scales. And for a small number of radical prime mov-
ers, idealism has *become* their greatest interest; it
serves thus as an igniting spark for the self-interest of
the mass.

That white Southerners value money is not just evidence that they share the general ambitions of American society; it explains why desegregation has been
accomplished in a number of crucial areas, even in the
Deep South. The profit motive is often stronger than the
segregating motive, and race relations groups, sometimes unconsciously, sometimes very deliberately, have
played upon this fact.

The boycott is the most direct proof that money
ranks high enough in the value-hierarchies of Southerners to weaken their traditional determination to maintain a segregated society. Bus companies in various
cities, tradesmen in Tuskegee and Atlanta, have un-

abashedly made turnabouts in their actions toward Negroes after boycott campaigns.

This power of economics works itself out in odd ways in the ordinary business of daily work in the South. A white plumbing contractor will hire a Negro helper and sit beside him on the front seat of his half-ton truck rather than hire a white helper and pay him ten dollars more per week. The wage differential accounts in thousands of instances for the hiring of Negroes instead of whites, even though the two races must then sit or work together. A diligent statistician could probably work out the prevailing market price of segregation—it does not appear to be worth more than about ten dollars a week to the white Southern employer. Whites work alongside Negroes in factories and on construction jobs, not always in superior capacities, for the good old-fashioned reason that "it's my job." Segregation is not worth the cost of a job to most Southern whites.

Another proof of the power of economic pressures to break down racial barriers is the increasing amount of service being given to middle-class Negroes by white laborers. The old servant-employer relationship is being reversed as the Negro bourgeoisie expands. There are countless examples: the white telephone repairman wiping his feet as he enters the home of a Negro businessman; the white employees of a contractor digging ditches on the campus of a Negro university; the white deliveryman unloading his wares at the back entrance of a Negro lawyer's home. In every one of these cases, the simple value of "making a living" overrides whatever scruples these whites may have.

There are also side effects, of an educational nature,

to these reversal-of-role situations. An elderly white woman who taught biology at Spelman College was in the hospital recovering from an illness, and Spelman's Negro President and his wife came to visit her. When they had left, the white nurse on duty came into the room and asked her patient: "Those colored folks work for you?" The biology professor answered: "No, I work for them."

The high value placed on profit was illustrated neatly, and with a touch of irony, in a series of moves by the General Assembly of Georgia a few years ago. In the closing days of its 1959 session, the Assembly passed a resolution asking that six justices of the United States Supreme Court, headed by Chief Justice Warren, be impeached for having given "aid and comfort to the enemy" by their decisions. At the very same time, the Assembly quietly killed a bill passed in the Senate which would have banned inter-racial baseball and other integrated sports activities in Georgia.

Thus, on the one hand, Georgia legislators undertook an action of heroic proportions, a frontal assault on the Supreme Court of the United States. On the other hand, their initial determination to keep Negroes and whites from playing baseball together in Georgia buckled and collapsed, humiliatingly, with the retreat led by the same stalwarts who had just stormed, without hesitation, the judicial fortress of the Republic. It was a fascinating Jekyll-and-Hyde performance, which deserves to be described in some detail.

Chief Justice Earl Warren and Associate Justices Douglas, Frankfurter, Black, Clark, and Reed (the latter three, incidentally, Southerners) were cited for "high crimes and misdemeanors" in a resolution asking Georgia's congressmen to initiate impeachment charges. The proposal was drawn up by State Attorney-General Eugene Cook and was strongly backed by Governor Marvin Griffin. Carl Vinson, dean of Georgia's congressional delegation, ridiculed the idea, and other Georgia congressmen seemed embarrassed by it. Only the state's new Senator, Herman Talmadge, gave it definite encouragement.

In answer to a number of state legislators who privately considered the resolution a piece of nonsense and publicly declared their opposition, its sponsors said that it was "thoroughly documented." The "documentation," it turned out, consisted of a long list of civil-liberties decisions rendered by the Supreme Court that went back to the Thirties and the Forties, in which the defendants were accused of being subversives, as well as the Smith Act trials of the eleven top Communists. All of this was accompanied by enough volume-and-page citations from the U.S. Reports to swell the chest of any small-town lawyer. These decisions, in which one or more of the named justices had participated, were proof, the resolution declared, of "aid and comfort to the enemy" (a phrase taken from the treason-defining clause of the Constitution).

Some of the statements in the impeachment resolution turned out to be troublesome. One Georgia state Senator urged that the justices be "censured" rather than "impeached," on the ground that a too foolish move would simply hurt the segregation cause; he noted that "bribery" had been charged in the resolution against Justice Felix Frankfurter, on the ground that he accepted an award from the NAACP. The impeachment resolution, he pointed out, got its information about the NAACP award from *The New York Times* and the *Baltimore Afro-American*. How could defenders of segregation, argued the Senator, take the word of these two newspapers?

The sponsor of the resolution replied to these forensic jabs with stirring oratory. Segregation, he assured his listeners, as he looked straight up at some Negro college students leaning forward in the "colored" section of the gallery, was not at all the issue. The fundamental question, he insisted, was "states rights." (One could almost substitute the word "slavery" for "segregation" and be transported back to the arguments of a glorious civilization gone with the wind.) He then quoted, in swift succession, Thomas Jefferson and Attorney-General Eugene Cook to prove his point. The resolution, which had already passed the House by an easy majority, now carried the Senate with just a scattering of opposition. The modern day fire-eaters were happy.

The sports segregation bill was another matter. It did not involve long-range verbal artillery aimed at distant Washington, but hand-to-hand fighting, with cold cash, on nearby baseball diamonds. The impeachment of Supreme Court justices was a fantastic bargain that cost the state no more than the price of printing a wordy resolution, but the sports bill, the legislators soon realized, might cripple the lucrative baseball business in Georgia and cost the state millions of dollars.

Although there were no Negro ball players on Georgia teams, there were a dozen in the South Atlantic League, a Class A organization containing four Georgia teams. If the bill passed, teams with mixed racial composition from other states could not play in Georgia; this would mean the death of the League and the loss of huge sums of money by Georgia businessmen. In addition, farm teams maintained in Georgia by a number of major league ball clubs would probably have to move from the state, thereby eliminating another source of local income. And major league exhibition games would have to by-pass Georgia. As the bill drew close to a vote, the worried president of the Atlanta Crackers, one of the nation's leading minor league ball clubs, visited Governor Griffin, carrying with him expressions of concern from major league and minor league executives.

Griffin loudly maintained his purity of principle, but there was a noticeable growing uneasiness among legislators as the sports segregation bill, which had passed the Senate, came up in the House on the last day before adjournment. Administration spokesmen on the floor, while ostensibly holding fast to an ideology dearer than life itself, quietly handed shovels to those preparing to entomb the bill under an avalanche of amendments. A legislator from Savannah proposed an amendment, obviously designed to prevent enactment of the measure, which would have made it unlawful for whites and Negroes to live or work in the same city! Another moved to extend the integration ban to "picking or chopping cotton; suckering, priming, or grading tobacco, pulling or shucking corn, and threshing peanuts or processing eggs."

Clearly, the retreat was on, and when a motion was made to adjourn the legislative session within ten minutes, House Speaker Marvin Moate called a voice vote quickly and declared the Ayes had it. Senator Leon Butts, sponsor of the sports segregation bill, suddenly became lonely and commented with bitterness: "I think it's a shame the major league ball clubs and the NAACP have gotten control of the Georgia House."

Within twenty-four hours, the Georgia General Assembly had fallen from peaks of battle valor worthy of a Stonewall Jackson or a Jeb Stuart (not mounted on prancing horses, however, but lounging on legislative cushions) to something like the rout of bewildered Union soldiers at Bull Run. And it was no consolation to know that the defeat was administered not by guns but by dollars, that it was brought on, not by physical cowardice, but by "good business sense." The impeachment of six justices of the Supreme Court, so daring a venture as to thrill every arch-segregationist in the state, had turned out to be a Walter Mitty dream, disintegrating before the less exalted but more earthy vision of cash.

In the baseball segregation case, the pure love of sport itself played a very small part, and only indirectly, in that the existence of this interest in the population at large determines the profitability of the sport. But in other cases, it is an important factor. White Southerners will not allow segregation to interfere with a pleasurable activity involving sports or recreation. Georgia Tech students almost rioted some years ago when it appeared that segregation policies might cause cancellation of an important game. Today Negroes and whites mingle in Ponce de Leon Park, where the integrated Atlanta Crackers play; a baseball fan is more interested in who occupies first base than in who occupies the next seat.

People's *real* preferences—that is, in a living situation rather than in the artificial context of public opinion polls—are revealed in their actions. Since there is

no legal compulsion to attend theaters, movies, and per-
formances, there must be either a very strong personal or social need for such entertainment, or a rather
weak fixation for segregation; for white Atlantans did
not stop going to the opera, the movies, or concerts after
these were opened on a non-segregated basis to Negroes in 1963. To put it more accurately, the need for
entertainment is clearly stronger than the need for segregation.

In the spring of 1960, an unusual assault was made
by Negro students on the segregated municipal auditorium in Atlanta that called into play a whole complex
of the value-preferences of the white people who were
involved. The auditorium, a huge structure downtown,
is the main setting for musical shows, ballets, and the
Atlanta Symphony Orchestra. It long had a special section for Negroes.

At the time, the Atlanta-Morehouse-Spelman Players, a richly talented drama group drawn from faculty
and students in the Negro colleges of the Atlanta University Center, were rehearsing the musical show *Finian's Rainbow* for a performance at Spelman College.
The Atlanta student movement had just gotten under
way in a burst of sit-ins and jailings aimed at desegregating lunch counters. A committee of student leaders
in the movement decided one evening that, among
various segregated facilities of the city, the municipal
auditorium was one of the weakest pillars and should
be the object of a frontal attack.

A road showing of *My Fair Lady* was to open the
next day at the auditorium. What would be more fit-
ting, the students thought, than to have Negroes who
were themselves interested in the theater seek admit-

tance to *My Fair Lady,* unsegregated? An emissary was dispatched to the group rehearsing *Finian's Rainbow* to find willing participants for the project. Since students can rarely scrape up enough money to pay for theater tickets, several faculty members were asked to contribute. Henry West, the young white professor of philosophy at Spelman College, went downtown and bought tickets. The box office, of course, gave him tickets for the "white" section. They were up front in the orchestra, the best seats in the house.

Early the following afternoon, an unusual group of young people assembled on the Spelman campus to ride downtown to see a matinee performance of *My Fair Lady* at the municipal auditorium. All were theater personalities. All were impeccably dressed and remarkable-looking in their own way. There was the director of *Finian's Rainbow,* Dr. J. Preston Cochrane, Professor of Drama at Spelman, tall, powerfully built, a black-skinned and handsome Othello. With him was Ves Harper, a professor at Clark College, a genius of set and costume design as well as a talented dancer, slender, light-skinned, bearded. There was one of the actresses in the Atlanta University players, a vivacious and attractive Spelman student named Lenore Taitt (whom we shall encounter later in this book as occupant of a county jail in South Georgia) and a Morehouse student-actor whom everyone called Tex, six-foot-five, slim, mild-mannered.

When they arrived at the theater, the attendant took their tickets and tore them in half. He had already given them the stubs when he took a startled second look at the tickets. He said "Wait a moment, please" and ran for the manager. Armed with the ticket stubs, the group decided not to wait. They made their way into the auditorium, and a slightly bewildered usher conducted them to their rightful seats. White people sitting all around them showed slight signs of curiosity, but otherwise made no moves indicating either alarm or protest. A moment later, the manager appeared and asked politely if they would mind taking other seats, since this was reserved as a white section. Yes, they would mind, they said; the seats had been reserved for them, as their tickets indicated. Somewhat nervous, the manager said they were holding up the performance of *My Fair Lady,* for it would not be able to begin until they changed seats. They could wait, Ves Harper said gently.

The manager rushed back to his office to call city hall. He got Mayor William Hartsfield on the line, told him the situation, and asked for advice. The Mayor thought a moment, then drawled, "The only suggestion I can make is that you dim the lights." He hung up. The manager went out and gave the order for the show to go on. But he was still troubled by the fact that he was violating the city ordinance which said that the manager of the auditorium would designate certain sections for Negroes and others for whites. When queried later by the press, he replied that he had designated those orchestra seats occupied by the Atlanta University group as a Negro section, so everything was legal!

The newspapers that evening carried a front page story saying that Negroes had watched *My Fair Lady* from the orchestra. It was the beginning of the end for segregation at the municipal auditorium, and today there are no separate sections for whites and Negroes.

How low down segregation is on the list of personal

needs for many white Southerners is borne out by another situation connected with the showing of *Finian's
Rainbow* by the Atlanta-Morehouse-Spelman Players.
Imagine a twenty-year-old Southern white boy, out of a
small town in South Carolina, where his father is fore-
man of a textile mill. Atlanta is a big city for him. After
a year of college he arrives there, because of an intense
desire to be an actor, and begins taking small roles in
one of the little-theater groups around town. From
nine to five he works at some minor clerical job. Like
most Southern whites, he has never had more than cur-
sory contact with Negroes, and he has accepted the attitudes toward them that most Southerners have—neither hostility nor friendliness, but indifference, along
with a complete readiness to laugh in agreement at
anti-Negro jibes made by others, and perhaps to do
much worse, depending on the group atmosphere.

Would this young white Southerner seek an acting
role with a Negro drama group, directed by a Negro,
involving constant contact with Negroes, for an audience mostly Negro? He did, in this case. There was
no conscious awareness that with this act he was about
to change his whole life-viewpoint about the Negro.
The overwhelming impetus to his decision was that
here was a fine role in a top musical drama—the role
of the leprechaun Og in *Finian's Rainbow,* for which he
thought his talents were particularly suited, and they
were. But once drawn into the situation by his love for
the theater, he came into close association night after
night with a talented group of young Negroes (and a
few other whites who had knocked over the racial barriers years before) and went through the kind of
transformation which tears to bits all theories about ra-

cial "instinct." In the play he falls in love with a young girl—a role enacted by a beautiful, mahogany-skinned Spelman College student. If he had internal misgivings about going through the scene before a large mixed audience, he gave no sign of it. While driving him home one night after rehearsal, I listened to him talk with astonishment at what a new vision of people—black and white—this experience had opened to him.

The power of the immediate as opposed to traditional psychology's emphasis on the power of the individual past, and to traditional historiography's emphasis on the force of the social past—this has been thrust at me vividly again and again these years in the South. Keep in mind that I am talking now about *behavior,* not about *thought* felt or verbalized. I have seen the simple pressure of social courtesy, for instance, make people behave counter to the most insistent demands of their background and ideology. An avowed segregationist, in a room with Negroes for the first time, where everyone around him is shaking hands in greeting, is introduced to a Negro man. The Negro extends his hand. At that moment all the generations of prejudice behind that white man fall away before the overwhelming pressure to do what everyone else does. He shakes hands. I have witnessed that scene enacted a half dozen times, and its frequency is multiplying with geometric speed throughout the South—and the nation—as new situations of contact are created every day.

The Dobbs House Restaurant at the Atlanta Municipal Airport was the first one desegregated in that city. It was done in 1960 by a lawsuit, which was effective because the restaurant operates under a lease granted by the city and therefore has the public connection required before the "equal protection" clause of the Fourteenth Amendment can be invoked. At the trial in federal court, a chief witness for the city, fighting the desegregation action, was the restaurant's hostess. She was a woman whom I had seen many times at the airport restaurant, and who had responded rather curtly to a query about Negroes being served there. But after the court order to desegregate was issued, I went there with Negro friends many times, and she received us with a startlingly warm display of graciousness. The law compelled her now to admit Negroes, but not to encourage them to return by friendly treatment. What was her motive? Financial gain for the restaurant? A basic decency now released by legal sanction? Role-playing?

Of the various roles a person is expected to play in modern industrial society, there is no more demanding one than that of the *job*. Take an ordinary man, but a policeman's uniform on him, a badge on his chest, and a club in his belt, and he begins to behave differently. Elect a man to political office, and his personality changes. A boy leaves the farm and becomes a salesman, and the *role* now determines his personality. Success, status, and the job are probably the most important determinants of male behavior in this country.

This general truth helps illuminate, I think, what would otherwise be incredible—the dramatic changes in behavior of Southern white politicians during the rapid transformation of the South today. The aim of the politician is to win and hold office—and all other values are subordinated to this, including that of racial segregation. So long as the Southern political figure finds it politically advantageous to use racism, he does so. When it becomes more useful politically to speak in moderate or even liberal terms about race relations, he switches with admirable agility.

The rapid rise in Negro voting in Atlanta after World War II is attributable to the end of the poll tax, the stimulus of wartime slogans of equality, the existence of a Negro intellectual élite in the city which could supply leadership, and the occurrence of several election campaigns in which the issue of racial equality was sharply drawn. In 1946, after the outlawing of the "white primary," and the selection of a promising congressional candidate to run against arch-segregationist James Davis in the Fifth District, Negro leaders John Wesley Dobbs and A. T. Walden led a phenomenal drive which registered tens of thousands of Negroes in time for the primary. With this impressive rise in Negro voting, the Mayor of Atlanta since the 1930's, William B. Hartsfield, began to shed his old segregationist ideas and to befriend in a moderate way the Negro community. As a result, Negro voters in Atlanta, almost as a bloc, supported Hartsfield in his race for the mayoralty.

So long as Hartsfield's friendliness to the Negro was not too overt, he could also count on a substantial white vote, because of his experience, ability, and reputation. When Hartsfield became clearly identified as the favorite of Atlanta's Negroes, the issue became sharply drawn, and a question arose for political analysts: since Negroes were still only a minority of the voting population (roughly one sixth), could Hartsfield capture enough white votes, despite his clear identification with Negroes, to triumph over an avowedly racist candidate?

This question was answered clearly in 1957 when Hartsfield ran against one of Atlanta's most rabid segregationists, Lester Maddox. Maddox owns a restaurant called "The Pickrick," and advertises every Saturday in the *Atlanta Constitution,* which he abhors, through a personal column that is partly devoted to advertising Fried Chicken and partly to flailing away at integration, the United Nations, and Communism, with strong suggestions that all three are the same thing. Occasionally the two functions are combined, as in the following passage for one advertisement in 1962: "Special Tonight, Order of Pickrick Skillet-Fried Chicken, Delicious-Tasty-World's Best (Segregated, Too), Dark Meat 20¢, White Meat 40¢."

Maddox played to the hilt Hartsfield's endorsement by the Negro population, and there was genuine concern among Hartsfield backers about the effect of this on Atlanta's white voters. The results were informative: Hartsfield won, with virtually all of the Negro vote, and a substantial part of the white vote. Here were two opposing candidates: Hartsfield standing for experience, ability, proven excellence simply in terms of the progress of Atlanta; Maddox standing for a harder line on the race question. Most whites, faced with only these two choices, valued segregation above good government. But *enough whites* felt differently to enable Hartsfield to win.

By 1956 and 1957, consciousness of the Negro vote among politicians in the Atlanta area was already causing stark changes in behavior. White candidates who had ardently supported segregationist legislation in the Georgia General Assembly began showing up in Negro churches at election time, with wife and little ones, in the good old American political style. One legislator who had voted for the bill that called for impeachment of the six Supreme Court justices appeared at a leading Negro Baptist church to plead for support at the polls. Such changes in behavior are not superficial but may even be cumulatively reinforcing: two years later, this same politico introduced a bill in the Georgia state legislature on the eve of the school segregation controversy that asked for the removal of all references to segregation in the state Constitution.

Under Georgia's county unit system, nominees for office in Georgia were elected by "unit" votes in each county which were flagrantly disproportionate to the population of that country and thus ensured domination by the less-populated rural counties. In 1962, the courts abolished the system, and a political revolution was in the making. That year, former Governor Marvin Griffin, who had led one of the worst-managed administrations in Georgia's history, ran for office on a race-hating platform against Carl Sanders. Sanders was a moderate on race (meaning: segregationist, but not inflammatory, and showing signs of flexibility and change) and had a good record as a state legislator. Here too, *if* race was the supreme issue for the overwhelming majority of whites in Georgia, they had a chance to put Griffin in as governor. They did not. He went down in a decisive defeat.

If race-baiting were the supreme desire of white Georgians in the Atlanta area, Congressman James Davis, an old-time bitter-end segregationist and arch-conservative, would still be in Congress today. Back in 1946, with Negroes voting in large numbers for the first time, Davis's opponent for the Fifth District nomination, Mrs. Helen Mankin, received 53,000 votes to Davis's 43,000, but was defeated because Davis's votes had been concentrated in two counties that had a majority of the unit votes. In 1962, the county unit system gone, Davis lost to Charles Weltner, not an integrationist by any means, but a candidate far more friendly to the Negro community.

The conclusion to be drawn again and again from recent elections in the state of Georgia is not that white Georgians will vote *against* a racist because of that fact. It is, rather, that race is not *as important* to a significant number of voters as is a reputation for clean government and economic progress plus those prepossessing personality traits which seem to mean much to the electorate.

There is a profound lesson on human behavior in the remarkable change of posture by Governor Ernest Vandiver of Georgia during his tenure of office. In his Inaugural Address to the General Assembly on January 13, 1959, he said:

> They speak of "token integration." There is no such thing as "token integration." They know, or should know, that the few raindrops of "token integration" would become a downpour, a deluge and then a flood which would engulf our people. . . . I have been into almost every militia district of this state . . . there is a virtually unanimous opinion among the people of Georgia that the Constitution and laws of Georgia must be upheld to the letter. . . .
>
> The people of Georgia and their new governor say to the United States Supreme Court, that we

will fight it wherever it raises its ugly head, in these very streets, in every city, in every town, and in every hamlet—until sanity is restored in the land.

Exactly two years later, after a night of student rioting, and a firm court order for the admission of Charlayne Hunter and Hamilton Holmes to the University of Georgia in Athens, Governor Vandiver submitted to the court ruling and ordered state troopers to protect the two young Negroes. And in the fall of 1961, again in the face of firm court orders, he did not defy the court, did not "fight . . . in these very streets." Instead, he quietly went before the General Assembly and asked them to amend the Georgia Constitution to permit Atlanta to begin token integration of its public school system.

What were the considerations which in those moments of decision prompted Governor Vandiver, who had once vowed that no Negro children would go to school with white children while he was governor, to push aside his strong race feelings? We can guess at a few: the high-priority value of any chief executive playing his traditional role, to maintain law and order; a sensitivity to national public opinion somewhat greater than that displayed by a few other Southern governors; the possibility of his being selected for a job in the Kennedy administration (he had been strongly mentioned for a high post of near-cabinet rank in the Department of Defense).

The final embarrassment to the members of the Georgia General Assembly showed them not at all willing to commit hara-kiri. Voters in a new Atlanta legislative district, created out of a court-ordered reapportionment of the legislature, and mainly Negro, elected to the General Assembly a thirty-four-year-old lawyer, Leroy Johnson. He was the first Negro elected to the State Senate since Reconstruction days. With his inauguration in early 1963, those members of the Senate who had shouted out their defiance-to-the-death against integration would face a neat test of their own value-hierarchies: would they resign from the Senate in order to avoid sitting in the same chamber, eating in the same lunchroom, serving on the same committees, as Leroy Johnson? The answer hardly needs to be given.

Keeping in mind Governor Vandiver's quiet submission to court orders, it might be well to note that by far the overwhelming majority of white Southerners will not go to jail to prevent integration. Scenes of violence and brutality in certain places have given many Americans a false impression about the white South. Actually, only in a small percentage of the places where integration has taken place has violence occurred; mob leaders have been able to enlist the aid, in most cases, of only a small percentage of the population. Just a handful of hooligans can create a mob scene, and they have not been able to sustain such violence for more than a few days.

Even the murderous rioters at Oxford, Mississippi, after the registration of James Meredith, although they undoubtedly commanded much sympathy from the student body, were at their core a minority and stopped overt resistance rather than face jail. The Southern white may not like the Negro in his school—but he will not go to jail to prevent it. Ralph McGill's constant— and successful—exhortations to his fellow Southerners to "obey the law" regardless of their feelings was based on a shrewd estimate of his fellow man. Governor Wallace of Alabama and Governor Barnett of Mississippi, whose rhetoric was aflame with defiance, and who swore they would fight to the end, defined "the end" as somewhat short of going to prison, for when the showdown came, they both surrendered.

The tendency to commit violence is probably, for most members of a mob, a temporary emotional outburst rather than a deep, self-sustaining commitment. A Negro colleague told me of a friend in graduate school, who confided to him that as a youth he had participated in a Chicago race riot designed to keep Negroes from moving into the Trumbull Park Housing Project. He had, in fact, at the height of the rioting, helped push a piano through a second story window down into the crowd. What I have called the power of the immediate can work both ways!

The indisposition of even extreme racists to risk prison or needless trouble is shown by the toothlessness of the once-terrible Ku Klux Klan in Georgia today. The old night-riding KKK is gone. That their old valor had fallen into a pathetic state was shown during the sit-in movement in Atlanta, when their response to student picketing was a counter picket line around Rich's Department Store. The sight of young vigorous Negro students marching parallel with a rather pitiable line of Klan adherents—how ordinary they seemed without their masks—indicated quite vividly that the KKK had come a long way, reduced from shootings and lynchings to peaceful picketing.

The old terrorizing of Negroes and "nigger-lovers" by the Klan has also taken a turn toward moderation.

Instead of house visits, they make telephone calls, filled with obscenity and threats but hardly as frightening as a pounding on the front door. Instead of kerosene-soaked, flaming wooden crosses, they now use electrically lighted ones, their final bow to the age of electronics. Several years ago, when some KKK members in Atlanta tried to place one of these bulb-covered crosses on the lawn of an Atlanta citizen, they had to give up the project because they couldn't find an electrical outlet! That the Klan consists essentially of men without an outlet has been expressed in various ways by observers of the Southern scene, but never so graphically as by the Klan itself that night.

I am not saying here that Southern white violence is dead. Far from it: brutality, either actual or imminent, hangs over the Negro in the Deep South every moment of his life. What I *am* saying is that the containment of violence in certain parts of the South—like Atlanta—proves that it can be done elsewhere. Most white Southerners, strong as their feelings may be about race, will not behave violently. The violent ones are most likely to act when they know that the operating police power sanctions it. That is why the continuance of violence in the Deep South—and I will say more about this later—depends on local political leadership, and failing that, on the will and determination of the national government.

In a large group, the complex variety of value-structures among its members may create opportunities for a change in the situation. Although the value of social peace—of "law and order"—ranks high in any group, to be utilized for social change this attitude must be focused by a small leadership. That leadership may be motivated by a desire for crass political or economic gain, or for the establishment of human equality.

There has always been a handful who cherish human equality in that stronghold of Confederate tradition, the University of Georgia at Athens. But it took the riots attending the entrance of Charlayne Hunter and Hamilton Holmes to combine the feelings of these few with the desire of many others for social peace to create an effective counterforce to violence. Never before had "liberal" opinions emanated in any organized form from the university. After the rioting, four hundred of the approximately five hundred faculty members at the University met in the University chapel.

About three hundred of these faculty people signed a resolution which insisted that the two Negro students, who had been suspended by the University after the rioting, be returned to class and which urged that "all measures necessary to the protection of students and faculty and to the preservation of orderly education be taken by appropriate state authorities." The resolution said: "Let the governor of this state, its law enforcement officials and the people know that we, members of the faculty of this great institution, will not retreat from the responsibility of standing steadfastly by the rules of law and morality."

The desire for education is higher, among most college students, than the insistence on segregation. Clearest proof of this is the infinitesimally small number of students, none or close to none, who leave a college when it becomes integrated. Although some University of Georgia students demonstrated against Charlayne Hunter and Hamilton Holmes, it turned out that the riots had been sparked by non-students, including Klan

members and deputy sheriffs. Few students urged that
the university be closed to prevent segregation, and
2,770 of them out of a total student body of 7,000
signed petitions to the governor to keep the university
open despite integration. If actual behavior, as I have
suggested earlier, is more crucial than verbal response,
then the continued attendance of the students was even
more significant than the number of petition signers.

Surveying the dozen or so areas of peaceful, if token,
desegregation in Atlanta these past few years, we can
make these observations about the value-preferences
of white Southerners, in the mass: they will not stop
using the bus because Negroes are sitting near them;
they will not desist from having a meal at a desegregated restaurant if they are hungry; they will not stay
away from a movie, a play, a sports event, the opera,
because Negroes are sitting where they please in the
audience; they will not resign from an organization
once Negroes are admitted; they will not pull their
children out of a public school because Negro children
are in the same class; they will not vote overwhelmingly
for a racial supremacist if he also has other qualities as
a politician which they dislike; they will not stop
using the public library because Negroes are there.
In short, for a crucially large number of Southern whites,
segregation is not as important as any one or a combination of the following: economic profit, political
power, good government, an absence of violence, food,
recreation, an education, keeping a job.

Furthermore, there is also the powerful force of conformity, both to society at large and to close friends

and associates. Conformity is a favorite target of intellectual disdain; few liberals will confess that it is not
conformity in the abstract which they abhor, but conformity to certain values which they find reprehensible.
Liberals would be delighted, for instance, to have conformity to the principle of free speech. And there is a
world of difference between conformity to racism and
conformity to the idea of equality. The tendency of
people to seek security in the approval of their peers
and superiors can be used as a great moral weapon as
well as a divisive tool.

For a long time, race progress in the South had to
battle against the fact that all of the powerful influences
—the opinion-makers in politics and economics and the
mass media—supported a segregationist ideology
which stifled free expression of equalitarian ideas. Now,
fresh air is seeping in to ventilate the ideologies of the
past. While the mass of white Southerners are still attached to traditional belief, strong and influential forces
in Southern life are beginning to change the atmosphere. For one thing, white Southerners now feel the
scrutiny not just of their neighbors but of the rest of
the nation, indeed the rest of the world. More Southerners travel to other parts of the country, to Europe
and Latin America and Asia, and return with new out-
looks. More foreign-born and more Northerners come
into the South either as visitors or as residents. These in-
fusions have already begun to have an effect. Sons and
daughters of the South are going to Northern universities, or to liberal and desegregated Southern universities. People are watching national television programs, reading national magazines. Though they are
still a minority, among more and more Southerners it is

becoming acceptable to take a moderate, even a liberal stand on race relations.

The behavior of crowds illustrates dramatically that people, whose personal histories vary widely, behave in exactly the same way when confronted by a common, powerful, immediate influence. I have seen several hundred white people in Atlanta who came to a Negro college to hear a favorite folk singer—their farthest reach toward racial liberalism—caught up in the spirit of his singing, and joining hands with Negroes and whites near them to sing "We Shall Overcome," the battle song of the student sit-in movement. Five minutes later, perhaps a little shaken by the experience, they might have left the auditorium wondering how in the world they could do this. But at that one moment of common response they did as everyone else did—as the *situation,* rather than instinct or tradition, demanded.

Even stronger than the need to conform to society at large is the need to meet the approval of a few people whose influence—consciously or unconsciously felt—is potent and continuous. This may be a wife, a parent, a friend, an employer, an associate at work, a teacher, or a combination of several of these. The importance of role-playing in the behavior of the individual comes mainly from this small-group conformity, since any improper enactment of the role will come to the attention of one or more of that small circle of influential people. And as the number of people in society increases whose own expectations of good behavior include equalitarianism in race relations, there is a geometric increase in the number of other people affected by these new expectations.

A woman from a distinguished old Georgia family

—replete with Daughters of the Confederacy tradition, ancestry back to the Revolution, Negro servants,
and old-South attitudes of aristocracy and white supremacy—found herself involved several years ago in
a sharp conflict of roles. Her husband was dead. Her
son, a graduate of a large liberal Southern university and
of a Northern theological school with a reputation for
liberalism, decided to take a position teaching at Spelman College. That her son was going to teach in a Negro college came as a profound shock. That he also decided to take an apartment on the campus, with his
wife and their little son, was an additional blow.

My colleague asked me to his apartment at the start
of the school year to a little social gathering. He told
me he had invited his mother, as well as several Negro
faculty members and the college president, also a Negro. When I entered his living-room, I saw his mother,
elegantly dressed, walk up to the couch where the president and his wife were sitting, extend a tray of cookies
to them, and ask pleasantly if they would like some.
For that moment at least, her role as mother and as a
traditionally gracious Southern hostess in her son's
house, was dominant. It had pushed aside her history-
rooted role as a white lady of the old South, whom it
would be impossible to imagine attending a social
gathering with Negroes, let alone serving them.

I cannot leave the topic of value-hierarchies without
succumbing to the temptation to comment on children.
It is accepted quite generally that Southern children
need to be *taught* to shun Negroes—that their natural
tendency is to play with other children regardless of
color, which appears to them a minor curious difference, because they value play and companionship more

than anything else. The artificial value of racial identity has to be imposed on children to become potent, and the following story, trivial as it is, underlines this idea.

The three-year-old son of the Spelman professor of whom I just spoke was the first white child in the Spelman College nursery, which trains students in preschool education. At Christmas time each year the nursery school children were taken downtown to Rich's Department Store, where each would sit on Santa Claus' lap and whisper in his ear what he or she wanted for Christmas. Santa was a white man in need of a job, not loathe to hold Negro children on his lap—a combination of Christmas spirit and role-playing perhaps. When my friend's son came to his turn, he climbed on Santa's lap as everyone else had done. Santa Claus stared at the boy, looked around at all the other children, and back again at the boy on his lap. Then, instead of asking his customary question "What would you like for Christmas?" he whispered, "Boy, you white or colored?" The nursery school teacher stood by, listening. The little boy answered: "I want a bicycle."

Value-hierarchies help explain, I believe, the altered behavior—or the possibilities for it—in the great majority of Southern whites whose upbringing and ideology are strongly pro-segregation. But this emphasis does not do justice to another truth about the whites in the South, one which, even if it only applies to a tiny minority, challenges in its own way the mystique of incorrigible prejudice. I am speaking now of the existence of a very small, courageous, and growing band of white Southerners who need not be induced to change their behavior by the promise of economic or political advantage or the pull of conformity, because *their* value system includes, near the very top, the ideas that all human beings are fundamentally the same and that color should be eradicated as a basis for distinction in society.

I have personally encountered hundreds of such people in my small circles of activity in the Deep South, and there must be many, many more. The radioactivity of their influence is far greater than their numbers would indicate. A few were brought up in the North and came to live in the South; most however were born and bred in the Deep South.

A few random samples: a fiercely outspoken newspaperwoman and novelist from Macon, Georgia; another journalist from a small town in Georgia; a minister in a low-income, highly prejudiced neighborhood who ordered his assistants not to interfere with a young Negro girl who had come to services in his church; a small corps of young white Southerners who joined the faculties of Negro colleges; an Alabama boy who went through beatings and jailings to help the student non-violent movement in South Georgia; the students at the University of Georgia who extended friendly greetings to Charlayne Hunter and Hamilton Holmes. Besides those who have already crossed the line, there are the increasing numbers of white Southerners who are crossing it every day.

Every time we create a new situation of encouragement, another human being steps out of the shadows and comes forward. One autumn evening in 1961, my wife returned from a lecture on campus and with her was a young white girl of about nineteen, slender, shy, a student at Georgia State College who came from a small town in South Georgia. She had heard that an interesting lecture was being given at a Negro college on "the other side of town"; she became curious, and so, that evening, found herself sitting and listening in a mostly Negro audience. On the way out, she and my wife had begun a conversation, and then there she was in our living-room. We talked for a while, and she left.

We didn't see her again. In December, I traveled down into Southwest Georgia, to the city of Albany, in an uproar at that time after Negro demonstrations. At a mass meeting in a Negro church my first night in Albany, I listened to the chairman offer welcome to a group of students who had just been released from jail. They came down the aisle to the front of the church, and one of them was the slim, shy girl who had visited our house that night in Atlanta.

The white students at Emory University, of whom one or two had shown up in the early days of the sit-ins, soon began to get involved in larger numbers in "the movement." At a meeting of over a hundred Emory students one evening in the spring of 1963 I first met Rev. Ashton Jones, a tall, lean, smiling, itinerant white preacher in his late sixties, who was born in South Georgia. Rev. Jones had been beaten, kidnapped, and jailed over thirty times while walking and driving through the country with the message that all men are brothers. He spoke to the students at Emory that night (he was a graduate himself of Emory Divinity School) with such a zest for life, a joyful humor, that his listeners were not prepared for the occasional bursts of passionate indignation. At this writing, he has just been in jail for six months in Atlanta: the "hospitality committee" of the First Baptist Church called the police to evict him and several Negroes from Sunday services.

There is no end of surprises for those who see Southern whites as undifferentiated and hostile. On a Monday evening in May 1963, I received a call from Ralph Moore, chairman of the Atlanta student movement; he asked me to bring my car to the county jail to help return to campus forty students, who had been arrested the past week in a sit-in and who were being released that evening. In the jailhouse, along with Ralph and other students waiting for their friends to emerge, I saw a white woman, tiny, perhaps sixty years old, classically Southern with her white hair, pretty face, a little hat on her head. She was sitting on a chair quietly, alone. I wondered if she had a relative in the county jail, and wondered too what she was thinking of all those Negro students milling about her. A moment later I passed by where she was sitting and saw her talking pleasantly to Ralph Moore. He introduced me. She smiled sweetly: "My daughter is in jail. I do wonder when they will all come out. I'm so *proud* of her!"

It turned out that her daughter, like her mother born and raised in the Deep South, had just joined the English Department at Morehouse College and had decided to join her students in a sit-in. I remembered seeing her at faculty meetings, dark-haired, attractive, a Chaucer scholar getting her doctorate from Yale. We waited in the county jailhouse from 8:30 P.M. to 1:30 A.M. until the woman's daughter, with the last of the prisoners, emerged—and for that whole period her mother sat there, patient and good-humored. In the early abolitionist societies of the South, there must have been this kind of woman.

. . .

Everything I have said up to now is insistently op-timistic. This is because I want very much to be heard above the voices of those who say that discrimination is an unknowable maze in which we can only proceed slowly. I have tried to suggest that there are undreamed of possibilities for swift change which we can realize if we plan carefully and act boldly. Optimism, if based on realistic estimates, can be socially useful as a stimulant to action.

Cynicism may also be useful as a reminder of what remains to be done. And it is in this spirit of positive cynicism that we should remind ourselves that only the first shafts of light have pierced the Southern cellar.

There has been too much crowing to the nation about Atlanta and I do not want what I have said about *possibilities* to support the complacency of those who imply that overnight Atlanta has become a showplace of racial amity. In Atlanta and in the Deep South gen-erally, we have seen only the first tokens of a promised new order. The old society remains. A few Negroes are going to white schools; most still go to overcrowded, segregated schools. A few Negroes are becoming afflu-ent; most are miserably poor. The black bourgeoisie is buying new homes; most Negroes live in hovels. The signs are down here and there, but the idea that "Ne-groes aren't welcome here" is communicated in a thou-sand different ways. Negroes vote in Atlanta and a few other large cities, but not in the hundreds of towns that make up the Black Belt.

All of the encouraging changes that have taken place so far in the South are scattered shoots of green on a landscape which is still basically barren and ugly. What

I have sought is to dispel the notion that there is any mystical factor buried deep in the white Southerner which makes racial equality a hopeless dream. I have tried to do this by combining post-Freudian psychological theory and empirical observation to establish that Southern whites behave as everyone else does—that they are motivated by certain desires, influenced by certain pressures, which can be rationally examined.

Among the various theories which attempt to explain human behavior, I have claimed that those that emphasize the power of the immediate on the individual (the field theory of Lewin, the role-situation theory of Gardner Murphy, the interpersonal theory of Harry Stack Sullivan) are demonstrably more applicable to the behavior of the white person in the South than those which emphasize the drives of "instinct" or the overwhelming power of Southern history. That history itself, as C. Vann Woodward, Dewey Grantham, and others have shown, is more complex than the myth-makers have allowed. I have tried to show that in practice the white Southerner, like everyone else, chooses either consciously or unconsciously from a set of competing priorities, which are arranged in a hierarchy of preferences. And in this hierarchy, for the white Southerner segregation is almost never the supreme value.

The point of all this is not to sit back and wait, but to assume that responsibility which is conferred by understanding. It is true that the direction of change in the South is already set, and that all of the value-conflicts in people's minds will operate, even without conscious guidance, to produce a more equalitarian society. But the slowness of this process when not given impetus is shown by the deep persistence of prejudice as a mental attitude and by discrimination as a behavior pattern in the North. By conscious, deliberate use of the already existing value-structures in the minds of Southern whites, it is possible to move into high speed toward social justice and to wipe out in giant steps the cruelty already beginning to warp the lives of millions of dark-skinned children now growing up in this country.

The purpose of dispelling the mystique that hovers over the white South is to point out the possibilities for leadership. This leadership, to fulfill that great potential for change which waits inside the white man, must set out deliberately to create new situations everywhere in the South. It is true that you don't change *people* by administrative, legislative, or community power; but you do change *situations* by such power. This, by affecting the total field of influence surrounding individuals, brings alterations in behavior, and such changes in situation and behavior are the prerequisites for changing the ideas that people hold. The long-standing notion of liberals that integration will take a "long time" was predicated on the idea that "education" was the key to an equalitarian society. But the most perceptive theorists in the field of education—and John Dewey was one of these—recognized that new combinations of words poured into the ears have little meaning or effect until environments are transformed.

If the Deep South were not under the jurisdiction of the United States government in the year 1964, it would not be possible to speak so glibly about changing the situational environment of its people. In most parts of the world, at most times, those who recognize the need for social change do not have the power to effectuate it. The United States government does.

But although verbal recognition of this need has been expressed again and again, and although federal court decisions have cleared the legal paths, the executive and legislative branches move slowly and cautiously. "Politics is the art of the possible," the strategists endlessly intone. And because political leaders, schooled in *realpolitik,* make estimations of what is possible on the tacit hypothesis of their own caution, we get a self-perpetuating cycle of minimum action. White liberals in the North—and some Negro liberals—are trapped in the same cycle, and those white Southern leaders who have begun to recognize the need for change get neither the encouragement nor the guidance they need.

So far, all of these forces have had to be prodded by the Southern Negro demonstrating in the streets. He has not only the will to do this, but also some semi-conscious, pragmatic understanding of how to utilize the value-hierarchies of those holding him down. Our national leaders and that public which supports them, enthralled as they are by the mystique surrounding the white Southerner, have not seen the possibilities for faster social change.

Negro anger will make them see it in any event. But their perception will be sharpened—as will the vision of Southern Negroes—if that mystique is penetrated and pulled apart. Then the white Southerner will be seen for what he is: a member of the human race, with no special encumbrances that cannot be thrust aside in this moment of history, and with the capacity to take his place, tomorrow morning, in a more just society.

PART TWO

The "Mysterious" Negro

IN *The Southern Case for School Segregation,* newspaperman James J. Kilpatrick says that by "the South" he means the white South. There is a Negro South, he admits, but it is "mysterious and incomprehensible to most white men."

Some things in nature and society are mysterious because we do not yet have the means to decipher them, others only because we lack either the opportunity or the desire to study them. The mystery of the human being as a general phenomenon falls into the first category, for here we know as much as science can tell us at the moment and no more. The "mystery" of the Negro falls into the second category, because it is within our power to end his mystery *as a Negro;* whatever mystery remains is just that which he possesses as a human being. Here the limitations are not of science but of society. The Negro will be inscrutable until we begin to scrutinize him.

It seems hard for us to get into the marrow of our understanding that the behavior of Negroes is drawn from that same reservoir of possibilities which is the source of all human behavior. Every type of reaction shown by Negroes is found among people of all "races." A specific reaction may be caused in the Negro by actions that would bring different responses from others; this is because his personal history and his field of immediate environmental pressures are different. But *any* individual—outside of and beyond race—responds in his own way to stimuli, because of his own peculiar history, because of the uniqueness of his individual field.

Merely to understand that there is a reason for something, even without knowing the specific reason, is to end mystery. Mysteriousness comes from the belief, spoken or unconsciously felt, that something is unknowable. It is one thing to say that a Negro may react differently because of a different environment, past and present; for even without being able to extract the explanations from the environment, you know they are there. It is another thing to say, "Well, a Negro is a Negro, there's no figuring him out," which may be said just like that by some or in a more sophisticated way by others.

The Negro's anger is the same as any man's anger, his joy like any other's, his feelings of love like all feelings of love; his grief is drawn from wells of human misery sunk deep in every continent. To say that we cannot understand "how the Negro feels" is to say that we cannot understand how any other human being feels —that is, not *exactly*. But there are no feelings of the Negro that we cannot understand in significant degree, because they are all ours. The cause may be different, and the intensity may vary, but the quality is comprehensible to all humans.

The humiliation of the Negro can be felt by any man who has ever been humiliated, his anger by any man who has been angry. We can understand his hurt—though it may be deeper than ours—because we have all been hurt. Anyone who has captured a moment of joy in his life can imagine the intense joy of a great love. That is why artists have conveyed feelings stronger than those they felt themselves, and why some people can feel compassion for others.

We would be less than human then, if we did not have the capacity to understand "how the Negro feels." Hope for mankind rests on the fact that a human being has imagination with which to magnify even the faintest sensations which he has experienced. The point here is not that men *will* understand the Negro; the point is that men *can*. And if they can, the "mystery" of Negro behavior, which we conjured up on one forgotten night of fear, is something we made, and something we can dispel.

There are two things that make a person a "Negro": a physical fact and a social artifice. The Negro's physical characteristics (or the suggestion of such characteristics by his ancestry even if they are not actually visible) fit a type which has been arbitrarily defined by society, and society uses this definition for various motives of social profit as a pinpoint upon which to erect an incredibly complex structure of discriminatory action and belief. This fact and this artifice reverberate upon one another to create a unique history for the group. This history is then used as a basis for asserting some mysterious difference, beyond the physical. Each new wall built into the historical structure of race-consciousness contains a mirror which magnifies the original insignificant physical difference. When the walls collapse one day under the weight of indignation, the mirrors will break and physical difference will become what it is when unenhanced by social design: a petty visual fact, less meaningful for the real needs of society than differences in the colors of soil.

The mushroom cloud of antagonism that has been artificially created by man out of the original atom of physical difference is what we call race prejudice. It has long been considered one of the mysteries of human behavior. So long as it is considered mysterious and impenetrable, it will engender pessimism and will remain an excuse for inaction. If there is an unreachable something in men which we cannot fathom, then we must prepare ourselves for a long haul. The prophecy becomes self-fulfilling. The expectation of difficulty is paralyzing. For what incentive is there to proceed swiftly and boldly in the presence of a deeply ingrained and mysterious hostility?

Near the root of the mystery is our preoccupation with "cause." We keep asking what "causes" prejudice, and because we can never really answer that, we decide it is one of the imponderables of human existence. I am suggesting that "cause" as a general concept is one of those metaphysical conundrums like "God," which is made impossible of explanation by the manner in which we frame the problem. Causation, as a general phenomenon, is impossibly complex and elusive. But if one turns from a desire to establish intellectual certainty to a simpler, yet more important objective—changing a particular facet of the social order—then another possibility asserts itself. This is: to isolate from the great knot of causation any one thread which, if grasped, loosens the whole. In other words, to find any cause—even if it is not *the* cause, even if it does not exhaust all the possibilities of causative investigation—which, if operated upon, changes the result.

For race prejudice, that operable cause can, I believe, be stated: it is separation on the basis of inequality. Or, to put it another way, the universal detergent for race prejudice is *contact*—massive, prolonged, equal, and intimate contact.

Physical difference in itself is not sufficient to produce race prejudice; another factor is needed. This may be one of a number of things: economic profit, political gain, or the existence of almost any problem in the environment of the white man. It is an *x* factor, with a wide variety of possible substitutions. (It is exactly because the possibilities are infinite that no one can find *the* cause.) This *x* factor is so chameleon-like as to be virtually impossible of elimination; that is, a man could stub his toe in the presence of a Negro and develop race prejudice. And the physical difference, despite skin whiteners and hair straighteners on one side, and suntan lamps and hair curlers on the other, will remain (at least until intermarriage increases significantly). Thus it is not possible to eliminate the deadly combination—physical difference plus *x*— which produces race prejudice, by eliminating either one of the two in an *absolute* sense. So long as there is outstanding physical difference (and this may be either visually obvious or socially ordained when it is not obvious) the possibility for the birth of race prejudice will always exist.

Physical difference, however, can be eliminated in a *relative* sense. That is, skin color and facial features can become lost in a mass of other characteristics— qualities of both physique and personality—so as to lose their specialness as identifying features. Those physical characteristics which denote "race" become relatively insignificant when competing for attention with a hundred other aspects of personality. To create such a situation, segregation—both the legal segregation of the South and the actual segregation of the North—must be ended. When the Negro is separated as a group from the rest of society, he cannot be known in all his complexity. Only one thing is known about him for sure in this state of separation: he is a Negro. And this fact, dominating all else, becomes the causal explanation for every other aspect of his behavior.

The more contact there is between whites and Negroes, the vaster the number of sense impressions that flow back and forth, the more the physical characteristics which denote "race" become diluted in a sea of impressions of all kinds. Then, being dark-skinned, or having thicker lips or a softer nose, becomes as minor an object of attention as the fact that someone is short or has freckles or is a Baptist. Then, even if the sense impressions are bad ones, even if two people find they are incompatible, the grounds are no more sought in "race" than they are in shortness or freckledness.

But such contact must be massive, it must be equal, and it must be unrestricted. Race contact in neither the North nor the South has met these requirements. In the North, "integration" has meant a few Negroes in a dominantly white situation, where they are treated with something short of equality, where race-consciousness remains high because of their isolation, and where contact stops at the edge of the school playground or at the doorway of the job because of social and housing segregation. In the South there is more extensive con-

tact; large numbers of Negroes are visible in Southern
towns, on the streets, in the stores. But to the white
Southerner they appear as blurred shadows, almost as
if they were on the other side of a pane of glass. Where
there is individual encounter with Negroes in the South,
it is employer to employee, housewife to maid. Generations of white Southerners have deluded themselves
into thinking that in this way they got to "know" Negroes. Negroes joke among themselves, with just a hint
of bitterness, about this. In Atlanta one evening, I
heard Rev. Samuel Williams, professor of philosophy
at Morehouse College, tell a laughing Negro audience
in church that the governor of Georgia "gets his knowledge of the Negro from the kitchen."

Is there any place in the world where massive and
equal contact exists among the races? Some places in
Latin America come close to this ideal. An Atlanta
friend of mine took his family on a trip to Mexico. They
drove through Texas all night without stopping, because
they couldn't find a place that would take Negroes. He
told me afterward: "When we got across the border it
was like being in a new world. I can't express to you
what a marvelous feeling it was—just the simple feeling
of being free, being a human being."

A white professor of French—a man who had sur-
vived the Nazi concentration camps and who has lived
in many parts of the world—said to me after a short
holiday in Mexico: "Why do I love Mexico? I'll tell you
one thing, just one thing. When I returned from Mexico City to New Orleans, I took a cab at the airport and
said to the driver, to make conversation: 'New Orleans,
it is a nice city.' Do you know what he said to me?
'Yeah, except for the niggers!'" My mild-mannered

and cultured friend told this with an anger I had never seen in him. Then he smiled: "In Mexico, you see everyone together, black and white and café-au-lait, and who-knows-what-color, and who cares?"

In the United States, there is no comparable phenomenon. Here and there across the nation are tiny samples of such a society, where people of various colors mingle. Perhaps in some parts of New York City and San Francisco and a few other metropolitan centers, where people in the arts—musicians, actors, writers—gather. Perhaps in Harlem, or Bedford-Stuyvesant, at the fringes of all-Negro neighborhoods, where whites and Negroes live as cordial neighbors. But even in these pockets of resistance to the dominant American psychology, the loss of race-consciousness is sporadic, uncertain—because just around the corner is everyone else.

Among these rare oases in our country are the Negro colleges, where black and white and in-between live and work together. In the Atlanta University Center for many years, white people have been on the faculties, not only working there but making their homes in the heart of the Negro college community. I found that on the Negro campus, surrounded as it is by the traditional South, we slid back and forth across the border of race-consciousness. There were times when one could forget altogether about "race"; and then, without warning, it would snap a thread delicately spun. At recurring moments through the years, a voice would break into the conversation: "When are we going to stop talking about race!" But in those moments, hours, days, when we related to one another simply as human beings (or rather, complexly, as professors of French or English or biology, as married or single, as conservatives or liberals, veterans or newcomers) we caught a glimpse, at least, of the future.

I am speaking here of "integration" as opposed to "desegregation." You have desegregation when the legal bars to racial contact are lifted. You have integration when that contact actually takes place. Determined political leadership in our society can desegregate the entire nation and thus can create the possibilities for massive, equal, prolonged contact, which can then begin to eliminate race prejudice. To change people's *situations* is to change their behavior, in order eventually to change their minds. This requires, as a first step, legal desegregation. Then, with each opened-up area, people must pour in together and, like an army after a town surrenders, must actually occupy it.

People cannot be forced to have close contact with one another. But we can create situations where it is first legal, then possible, and finally without social stigma. Once artificial barriers are down through legal and extralegal means in housing, in employment, in schools, in marriage, the process, partly natural and partly planned, will grow with increasing momentum. Then, perhaps in the generation now being born, race prejudice will exist only in small vestigial pockets where one day it will decay and perish from sheer neglect.

The requirement of *massive* contact is arrested by the Deep South's current legal strategem: technically to obey federal court orders while maintaining the basic features of segregation. This is "tokenism," the artificial creation in the South of that situation which exists in so many places in the North—a single Negro in a white classroom, a handful of Negroes in a school for thousands, an occasional Negro employee in a huge organization. In Atlanta, when the schools were desegregated by court order in the fall of 1961, several hundred Negro students applied. They went through batteries of tests and interviews, as if they were being screened for a rocket flight to the moon. Ten students squeezed through this and were parceled out in twos and threes to be lost among thousands of white students at their respective high schools. Atlanta and other Southern cities call this, officially, euphemistically, "pupil placement." The result: isolation, fear, tension. White children thus get a glimpse of a Negro in the corridors, perhaps in their classes, but under such unnatural conditions as to make almost impossible any real human encounter.

Defending token integration, moderates, liberals, and politicians see it as a "first step" and as a way of making desegregation palatable to queasy stomachs in the white South. Against this is an array of arguments led by the simple demand of honesty, for behind the dutiful giving of tests by the professional educators to make sure the entering Negro student will "fit in" is the political need to claim a bulwark against the integrationists. Both the selection process itself and the result (one or two Negro children in an overbearing white mass) guarantee no one will "fit in." The climate of artificiality created by the battery of tests (which no white boy or girl, however mentally or emotionally deficient, is required to endure), the elaborate preparations for *the day*—all set up, in the end, a barrier against human intercourse. They delay indefinitely the kind of natural contact, in large numbers with no peering supervisors, which young people develop among themselves after some momentary initial feeling-out, and which in the long run, by erasing gradually the mental strain of race prejudice, is the only thing that can guarantee successful school desegregation. Boards of Education, constantly lecturing about the need to teach "values" to the young people of the United States, omit courage, by example, from the list, wherever they hold to the hypocrisy of "token integration" or "pupil placement."

Not many white people in the United States have had the opportunity to work and to live over a period of years with their wife and children in a predominantly Negro community. I count myself lucky to be one of these. This kind of total immersion is not just educational, in the pallid sense of booklearning; it is transforming, as real education should be. That is why the white students who have come to Spelman on exchange for a semester have not just exchanged schools and cities, they have undergone a personal revolution. They will never again be the same.

To exchange white America for the predominantly Negro world is to introduce a galaxy of new impressions. Those who have lived all their lives among whites, with an occasional awareness of an individual black or brown person, with only that vague consciousness most white people have of a dark mass of people existing around the corner or across town or across the ocean, have been deprived, sensuously speaking. I say this not to romanticize the Negro. His color-range is no "better" than the white, nor more beautiful; for "good" and "beautiful" transcend the question of color; his range is richer, more varied, however, so that to perceive it at close range is a magnification of sense experience.

The human race, through intermarriage, has developed a wide spectrum of skin colors and physical types. In the United States unfortunately, we have built a wall in the midst of the population and have put the largest assortment of colors on one side of that wall. On the "white" side, where skin color varies in a much narrower band, there is more variety in the yellows and reds of hair, the blues and greens of eyes, than among Negroes. So I am making no attempt here to glamourize the Negro as being special, but only wish to point out that each race, by separation, is denied (among many other more important denials) the sense-pleasure that accompanies an enrichment of visual experience.

A white woman who came to teach at Spelman College, after she had lived for three months in a dormitory for Negro girls, said "My notion of 'beauty' has changed enormously." In the United States, many whites grudgingly or not, will concede the existence of "beautiful" Negro women, but most often, these are the Negro women who closely approximate "white" conceptions of beauty: fair skin, straight or slightly wavy hair, Anglo-Saxon features. "Beauty" is intensely subjective, emotional, elusive, and it seems to me it is something above and beyond anatomical formulas; it can be perceived, or rather *felt,* in any human being regardless of physical characteristics. What happens, however, is that conventional notions of acceptable physical type act as a barrier against that spontaneous flash of feeling which races across space from another human being and says to us "This is a beautiful person." When contact has melted all barriers, that sensation will come to us from any color of skin, any facial or body type. With artificial restraints gone, the awareness of beauty can become truly personal rather than conventional.

It is the social effects of contact that are even more important. Those who argue the "deep roots" of prejudice shake their heads at the notion of swift change. But they do not really understand how quickly our consciousness of color can be transformed under a shower of sense impressions which is continuous over a period of years, or even months.

During a teacher's first weeks standing before a class of twenty or thirty Negro girls, a few faces, bright, inquiring, articulate, separate themselves from the mass. As more weeks go by, the mass itself breaks into distinguishable beings, clearly delineated not only in appearance but also in intellect and personality. After a while, there is no consciousness of color, only of individuals. Awareness of color pushes itself in from the world outside, as when some curious white person from "the other side of town" asks: "What are Negro students like?"

Negroes need contact too, to break down the picture they have of the white, as they see him from a distance: the picture of a man hostile to their every need. Girls from South Georgia and Mississippi and Alabama, who have never had any contact with whites except in perfunctory and subordinate relationships, come into class and see that their teacher is white. I have seen such students in my freshman classes, silent, withdrawn, looking at me warily as if to say: "Who are you and what are you doing here anyway?" Weeks or months later, it is different.

How swift a revolution can be made in the consciousness of both whites and Negroes through close contact is shown by the experience of that handful of white students who in recent years have come to Negro colleges as exchange students. A white girl from North Central College in Illinois, who came down to Atlanta to spend a semester at Spelman, said: "I registered for a course at Morehouse College, and when I walked into the class for the first time and saw all those dark men, I was terrified." The fear of the strange, along with the powerful American tradition of racism, and the mystique surrounding the Negro in the minds of white Americans, all combined to make that first encounter unsettling. "But soon everything changed. They were so wonderfully nice to me. And some of them became close friends of mine."

These exchange students are girls who come mostly from white communities where Negroes are rare. There is first the shock of finding oneself in a totally different visual environment, where everyone around is some shade of black or brown, with facial structures and hair types different than those of Anglo-Saxon Americans. Then the bombardment of the senses begins, with the slow changing of the inner mental field, until the Negro environment becomes as natural as the white environment once was. When suddenly among white Anglo-Saxons again, one becomes aware, as the Carleton girl on exchange at Spelman put it, of "all those pale faces and sharp noses." Contact—intimate, massive, and more than momentary—reshuffles all sensory memories and dissolves the mystique built upon the physical characteristics of the Negro.

These student exchanges have their effect also on the white people of the community, whose traditional images become assaulted by new sets of visual experiences. The Southern white is accustomed to seeing an all-white group from within, an all-Negro group from outside. He is also accustomed to seeing Negroes and whites in the mass, intermingled on streets and in department stores. However, when he sees a Negro and a white together, he finds certain predictable patterns: the nursemaid and the baby; the porter and the employer; the maid and the matron; the waiter and the diner; the laborer and the supervisor. In the past few years, with exchange students at Negro colleges in Atlanta and elsewhere, with white college students joining the Southern protest movement, new combinations have appeared. It is disturbing at first for the white Southerner to see a white and a Negro girl, both dressed in college clothes, around the same age, obviously interested in one another, walking together in the local shopping district. As it happens again and again, the shock vanishes, the old expectations become blurred, new ones are born.

So far, it is only a small number of Southern whites who are experiencing this revolution in perception. But the phenomenon is growing. The removal of legal obstacles to contact will speed things up. And as whites find Negroes living on their streets, working in their offices, showing up at their churches, the number of new person-to-person combinations will expand. The process has only begun, but its growth is likely to be rapid.

When that first semester of student exchange was over, I took two white students to the bus depot to return home. Accompanying them were the two Negro girls who had been their roommates. As they boarded the bus, the exchange students and their roommates embraced. The white bus driver stood watching in the doorway, incredulous, and almost unconsciously he said, out loud: "Well, I'll be damned!" Without doubt, the damnation will grow.

Color consciousness is relative. A black drop of ink on a white paper is startling, but when you begin filling the paper with other things, the drop becomes lost, though it is as black as before. And when the blackness or whiteness of skin becomes just a small part of many other, more relevant elements piercing our consciousness, it takes its deserved minor place. A Negro seen casually at a distance is mainly a black person. A Negro *known* is a person with dozens of different characteristics, one of the least important of which is blackness.

I became aware of how color consciousness is obliterated by a surrounding stream of other impressions when I once attended a play in which Negroes and whites were cast in their roles without regard to color. The family about whom the play was written had a light-skinned Negro woman as mother. A white boy played her son. A Negro played another son. For the first ten minutes of the play, we were all acutely aware of this. After the play became crowded with so many other problems and impressions, consciousness of skin color receded; on stage was just a family.

The stage, even in the Deep South, may soon become an instrument for dissipating racial awareness. But the first step in the process is a startling one; it is a kind of shock treatment, with an initial flare-up of racial emotions which gradually subside and then vanish.

In the spring of 1959, the talented Atlanta-Morehouse-Spelman Players presented the musical *The*

King and I. It was a magnificent production; the ballet
sequence based on *Uncle Tom's Cabin* was breathtak-
ing in its grace, color, and pounding emotion. In the
role of the King of Siam was Johnny Popwell, a Morehouse College football captain with a long string of acting credits, a handsome, powerfully built young man
with glistening black skin. The English schoolmistress
who came to tutor his children clashed constantly with
him while a mutual affection developed between them.
This was Anna, played by a blue-eyed, fair, and lovely
woman—my wife Roslyn.

As usual, the audience was mixed: white people from
the Atlanta community and Negroes connected with
the colleges. But this was the first Atlanta production,
so far as anyone could remember, with so many whites
in the cast: Anna, the English ambassador, several of
the King's many children. When the orchestra in the pit
began to play "Shall We Dance," the black and fierce-
looking King of Siam moved close to the white woman
schoolteacher. The audience was absolutely silent. He
put his arm around her waist and you could feel the
quick rise of tension in the theater. As the two danced,
the tension held for a moment, then slowly dissolved.
At a certain point the power of the music, the rhythm of
the dance, the total dramatic situation overtook and
smothered the initial shock of unexpected racial contact. The exact time of transition must have varied
from individual to individual, but it seemed to me that
the audience, captivated by the play, at some crucial
moment began to see an Asiatic King and a British
woman in a palace in Siam, and forgot, at least temporarily, that a black man and a white woman were
dancing together on a stage in Georgia.

In real life, all of us play so *many* roles; with closer

contact these will crowd out the artificially isolated one
connected with color-identity.

A well-done stage play, or a television program, de-
molishes the space between human beings and allows
you to *know* someone, even without person-to-person
contact. Millions of people lived for two hours with the
family in *Raisin in the Sun,* watching them wake up in
the morning, argue, laugh, dance, cry out in anger.

One can see the possibilities in the public appearance
of Negroes not *as* Negroes mainly, but as raceless enac-
tors of some necessary social role. In 1961, the Atlanta
University Center was given a weekly early-morning
period on a leading Atlanta television station to present
an educational program on Chinese civilization. One of
the first programs was a lesson in Mandarin, the chief
dialect of China. The program opened with the camera
focused on a white professor listening to a conversation
in Mandarin carried on by two people not visible on the
screen, who sat on either side of him. After a moment
the camera swung to one of them, a Chinese graduate
student at Atlanta University. Then it swung to the
other, a young Negro student at Morehouse College,
who had studied Mandarin at Yale and had been an Air
Force interpreter on Formosa. People who saw the program told me of the initial astonishment at seeing a Negro speaking Chinese. But, they said, as the program
progressed—in a matter of minutes—the fact of color
receded and the fascination of the Chinese language
dominated.

A few weeks later, Carl Holman, a Negro professor
in the humanities at Clark College, appeared on the
program to lecture on Chinese poetry. How relevant
was the "race" of a teacher to a listener captivated by

the words of Li Po, a T'ang Dynasty poet who wrote over a thousand years ago?

Those few white Americans who have had the chance to live in a predominantly Negro community have experienced that beneficent bombardment of the senses I have described. But so have many Negroes, particularly from the Black Belt areas of the South, who have never in their lives had close contact with whites. A Morehouse alumnus, with a doctorate in physics, told me about his freshman-year encounter with a white woman teacher. "She was a great teacher," he said "and also a fine human being, so provocative as a thinker. But most of all, I learned from her—wordlessly—that there was nothing mysterious about whites. She was the first white person I had ever gotten within five inches of, I mean in any important sense, and after a year in her class I just saw race in a way I'd never seen it before. That is, I saw it was *nothing*."

The more intimate the encounter, the quicker the erasure of impressions purely racial, and the more overwhelming those impressions that are simply human. Living together, working together, bring the fastest results in destroying race prejudice. And engaging in some common endeavor is an even more intensely productive experience.

The sit-in movement, which erupted in the Deep South in the spring of 1960, was a multi-pronged assault on the mystique of race. It brought a few whites, who joined the movement, into close and affectionate contact with Negroes. It brought young, attractive, intelligent Negroes—the finest examples of idealistic young Americans—before the public through television, motion pictures, the newspapers. And by opening lunch counters and other places for Negroes, the sit-ins constituted a pioneer assault on those barriers which inhibit the natural mingling of peoples in every-day life.

When a group of young Negroes "sat-in" at a Greensboro, North Carolina, lunch counter in Febru-ary 1960, the waves of excitement reached Atlanta. Two Morehouse men met in the Yates & Milton Drug-store, a regular meeting-place for students of the At-lanta University Center, and talked about Greensboro. Yates and Milton's was crowded with students drinking coffee and cokes. "You take one part of the store and I'll take the other, and we'll see if we can get people to come to a meeting." The Atlanta movement was thus begun. A Morehouse College student named Lonnie King became chairman.

Two groups sprang out of those early meetings. One, the smaller, was an "action" group. Influenced by CORE (Congress on Racial Equality), a national or-ganization which had long advocated non-violent di-rect action, these students began picketing Rich's De-partment Store downtown, demanding that Negroes be served at the various lunch counters in Rich's, asking too that Rich's hire employees on the basis of ability rather than color. The other group was larger and somewhat more conservative. It wanted to act, but the picketing technique seemed precipitous, and those asso-ciated with it were reputed to be "radicals." Yet, there was a growing, nagging feeling that talk was not enough, that the spirit of the sit-ins just begun in Greensboro, and catching on elsewhere, demanded some form of action. So, the larger Atlanta group, joined by those who had been picketing, began to talk and plan for a "sit-in" at lunch counters.

The college presidents of the Atlanta University Center became concerned. They apparently decided to try to cool the passions of the students somewhat, and called a meeting of leaders of the main student government, who might bring a restraining influence to bear on the hotheads. At this meeting, urging at least temporary postponement of sit-ins and picketing, the presidents offered a plan: first, to place a full-page advertisement in the Atlanta newspapers that would set forth the position of the student movement on segregation and bring to the attention of the white community the grievances of Atlanta Negroes. They offered, as an inducement, to help the students pay for it.

The students debated among themselves whether to accept the presidential proposal for an advertisement rather than immediate direct action. They decided to accept financial help, place the advertisement, and then follow it right away with action. And this is what happened. A Spelman student, just returned from a year in Paris, with the breath of freedom still inside her, wrote the first rough draft. Other students went over it, and it appeared March 9, 1961, on a full page in the *Atlanta Constitution* under a huge headline: AN APPEAL FOR HUMAN RIGHTS. Its impact on the city was sensational. Never before had Negroes addressed themselves so publicly, so boldly, without an ounce of humility, to the white community of Atlanta.

The appeal began:

We, the students of the six affiliated institutions forming the Atlanta University Center—Clark, Morehouse, Morris Brown, and Spelman Colleges, Atlanta University and the Interdenominational Theological Center—have joined our hearts, minds, and bodies in the cause of gaining those rights which are inherently ours as members of the human race and as citizens of these United States.

We pledge our unqualified support to those students in this nation who have recently been engaged in the significant movement to secure certain long-awaited rights and privileges. This protest, like the bus boycott in Montgomery, has shocked many people throughout the world. Why? Because they had not quite realized the unanimity of spirit and purpose which motivates the thinking and action of the great majority of the Negro people. The students who instigate and participate in these sit-down protests are dissatisfied, not only with the existing conditions, but with the snail-like speed at which they are being ameliorated. Every normal human being wants to walk the earth with dignity and abhors any and all proscriptions placed upon him because of race or color. In essence, this is the meaning of the sit-down protests that are sweeping this nation today.

We do not intend to wait placidly for those rights which are already legally and morally ours to be meted out to us one at a time. Today's youth will not sit by submissively, while being denied all of the rights, privileges, and joys of life. We want to state clearly and unequivocally that we cannot tolerate, in a nation professing democracy and among people professing Christianity, the discriminatory conditions under which the Negro is living today in Atlanta, Georgia—supposedly one of the most progressive cities in the South.

Among the inequalities and injustices in Atlanta and in Georgia against which we protest, the following are outstanding examples:

Then it catalogued, with irritating specificity, the wrongs committed against the Negro by the system of segregation in education, jobs, housing, voting, hospitals, concerts, movies, restaurants, law enforcement. It concluded with these words:

> We, therefore, call upon all people in authority —State, County, and City officials; all leaders in civic life—ministers, teachers, and business men; and all people of good will to assert themselves and abolish these injustices. We must say in all candor that we plan to use every legal and non-violent means at our disposal to secure full citizenship rights as members of this great democracy of ours.

Six student leaders signed: Willie Mays, James Felder, Marion D. Bennett, Don Clarke, Mary Ann Smith, Roslyn Pope.

Reactions in the white community varied. Mayor Hartsfield, a liberal and masterful politician, treated the "Appeal" with respect. But the Governor of the state of Georgia, Ernest Vandiver, denounced it. It is safe to say that none of the official pronouncements coming out of the Georgia Capitol in this century matched the Appeal for literacy or eloquence, to say nothing of moral values. Perhaps this infuriated the Governor. It was an "anti-American" document, he told the press. It was "obviously not written by students." Furthermore, the Governor said, "It did not sound like it was prepared in any Georgia school or college; nor, in fact, did it read like it was written in this country."

The Negro college presidents were happy, the Governor was unhappy, the Mayor was playing it cool, and the students were secretly preparing for action. On Monday evening, March 14, my wife and I were at a student party connected with the forthcoming production of *Finian's Rainbow,* when two leaders of the student movement told me the plans: eleven o'clock the next morning, ten cafeterias in downtown Atlanta, hundreds of students, a sit-in. They wanted me to telephone the press a few minutes before eleven, so as not to tip off the police.

Tuesday morning, March 15, about ten o'clock, six Spelman students came to our house on campus to borrow my car. They needed it, they said smiling, to "go downtown." About five minutes of eleven I started to call the press, but then decided not to take the slightest risk and waited until exactly eleven o'clock before calling. I could hear the editor on the other end of the telephone at the *Atlanta Journal* calling out assignments to reporters as I gave him the names of the cafeterias.

Seventy-seven students were arrested in the sit-in. There was no violence. Acting on legal counsel, the students had selected restaurants at city and county courthouses, lunch counters leased from federal buildings, and cafeterias connected with bus and train terminals, since all of these were covered, presumably, by the dictum that the Fourteenth Amendment applies to government-connected enterprises. Several hundred students had gone downtown, in small groups, and at the stroke of eleven had moved into seats in ten different cafeterias. Managers then called the police, who ordered the sit-inners to leave. By prearrangement, those students who were not prepared to go to prison left their seats, but the seventy-seven who stayed were hauled away to jail.

Five of the six Spelman students who had borrowed my car for the demonstration returned in the early afternoon. One, Marian Wright, was in prison. My wife fixed coffee and we all sat around in the living-room, the students talking spiritedly about their experience.

In a few days, the arrested students were out on bail, charged by Fulton County with three offenses: breaching the peace, intimidating restaurant owners, and refusing to leave the premises. With three-year sentences possible for each charge, this added up to nine-year sentences. The county prosecutor added to the seventy-seven sit-inners the names of the six students who had signed the Appeal for Human Rights. In addition, all were charged with "conspiracy," thus linking each participant to all ten restaurants and creating the theoretical possibility of ninety-year sentences! But, as we often told one another, nothing is fantastic in the state of Georgia. The cases were never brought to trial.

The sit-in movement that erupted in Atlanta in the spring of 1960 had an auxiliary effect: the revolt of some young Negroes against the tendency of the Negro college to imitate—even to exaggerate—American middle-class conservatism. There is a guard which many middle-class Negroes erect against the white world: a spurious sophistication delineated by Professor E. Franklin Frazier in his book *Black Bourgeoisie*. Working-class Negroes have their own kind of guard: silence, obsequiousness, or fury. Both traditionalism and pseudo-cultivation, however, are somewhat unsettled in the atmosphere of non-violent direct action against segregation; for such action brings the Negro, natural and militant and more "himself" than ever before, into direct and frank confrontation with the white world. The terrible thing about that black bourgeois guard—compassionate as we must be for the pain that brought it into being—is that it maintains, in its own way, the mystique of race which stands between white and black in this country.

Spelman College in Atlanta revealed, in the years of sit-ins and strife, this conflict between old and new inside the Negro world. At Spelman, there was always an emphasis on manners and morals, in the narrow sense. The Spelman girl was for generations the recipient of well-meant advice from her teacher-elders: be nice, be well-mannered and lady-like, don't speak loudly, and don't get into trouble. Spelman was pious and sedate, encrusted with the traditions of gentility and moderation. But with the sit-in movement, there began a revolt of Spelman students against these exhortations, against tradition itself.

Not that Spelman girls stopped being "nice"—they stopped being genteel only long enough to walk back and forth in front of two Atlanta supermarkets, with picket signs demanding an end to discrimination against Negroes. They were still well-mannered, but with this went their adherence to the declaration that they would use every method short of violence to end segregation. As for staying out of trouble, they were doing well until that March 15, 1960, when the great sit-in took place. Of the seventy-seven students arrested, fourteen were Spelman girls. The staid New England women missionaries who helped found Spelman College back in the 1880's would probably have been surprised at this turn of events, and conservatives in administration and faculty were rather upset. It looked at that moment as if respectability were no longer respectable among young Negro college women.

"You can always tell a Spelman girl"—alumnae and friends of the college had said for years. The "Spelman girl" walked gracefully, spoke properly, went to church every Sunday, poured tea elegantly, and in general had all the attributes one associates with the finishing school. If intellect, talent, and social consciousness happened to develop also, they were, to an alarming extent, by-products.

With the sit-ins, this began to change. It would have been an exaggeration to say, in the spring of 1960: "You can always tell a Spelman girl—she's under arrest." Yet the statement had a measure of truth.

Not only did Spelman girls participate strongly in all the major actions undertaken by students of the Atlanta University Center; they added a few touches of their own. White Atlantans, long proud that their "nice" Negro college girls were staying "in their place," took startled notice of the change. When a Spelman girl riding downtown on the bus took a seat up front, the bus driver muttered something unpleasant, and a white woman sitting nearby waved her hand and said: "Oh, she's prob'ly goin' downtown to start another one o' them demonstrations."

Even before the sit-ins, the reputedly sweet and gentle girls began to cause trouble. As early as January of 1957 they were challenging segregation. That year they aroused the somnolent legislators of the Georgia General Assembly into a near-panic by attempting to sit in the white section of the gallery. When the speaker of the house saw the young Negro women with one white and one Negro faculty member sitting in the "white" section, he seemed to develop a quick case of apoplexy and rushed to the microphone to shout: "You nigras move over to where you belong! We got segregation in the state of Georgia!"

Attendants hurried upstairs to enforce the order. The group quietly rose and, after a brief consultation, decided to watch the proceedings from the "colored" section, having already demonstrated their real desire. The presence of the white teacher (myself) with them in the "colored" section created much nervousness in the chamber below; the legislators, forgetting about the business at hand (a bill on trout fishing), craned their necks and stared. Not quite sure whether the teacher was a dark white man or a light colored man, they hesitated to order him out.

A footnote on the ironies of Southern courtesy must be added here. When the group was sitting, to the satisfaction of the speaker of the House, in the "right" section, he dispatched a messenger to find out who they were. Then, the information in his hand, he came to the microphone again and announced, as was apparently the custom with all visiting groups: "We hereby cordially welcome the students and faculty of Spelman College to this session of the General Assembly."

When the next session of the legislature convened in early 1958, Spelman students in the Social Science Club decided to pay another visit. Not ready yet, as they would be two years later, to go to jail, they decided to protest silently by standing in the white section. Again,

the House speaker dashed for the microphone, grabbed
it from a legislative orator, and demanded that the
group leave. The students filed out through the nearest
door, to the accompaniment of loud applause from the
legislators, who saw this as a military victory. But the
applause had hardly died down when the group re-
entered the gallery through another door and stood
near the colored section, maintaining their resolve not
to sit down in a segregated section.

It took several more attempts during subsequent legislative sessions, a march downtown, a dramatic picket
line circling the gold-domed State Capitol in the spring
of 1961, and the election of a Negro Senator to the legislature, to accomplish the desegregation of the gallery. When that day finally came in January 1963,.
Spelman students were in the gallery to mark the occasion, watching with an interest both personal and social
as Leroy Johnson, a Negro lawyer, placed his hand on
the Bible to take his oath of office. Three white Senators put their hands on the same Bible at the same time,
an act that might be considered revolutionary were we
not living in an age where the impossible takes place
daily.

Also before the sit-ins and before bus segregation
was declared illegal, some Spelman girls rode in the
front, withstanding the glares and threats of fellow passengers and the abuse of bus drivers. Once, a white man
pulled a knife from his pocket and waved it at one of
my students sitting opposite him in a front seat. She
continued to sit there until she came to her stop, then
got off. Spelman students spent hours between classes
at the county courthouse, urging Negroes to register for
voting. They made a survey of the Atlanta airport for

a suit to desegregate the airport restaurant, and a Spelman student took the witness stand at the trial to help win the case.

Such activities brought some bewilderment to the conservative matriarchy which has played a dominant role in the college's history. The twelve-foot-high stone wall, barbed wire fence, and magnolia trees that encircle the Spelman campus have always formed a kind of chastity belt around the student body, not only confining young women to a semi-cloistered life in order to uphold the prevailing conception of Christian morality, but "protecting" students from contact with the cruel outside world of segregation.

A similar barrier, more spiritual than physical, surrounded the entire Atlanta University Center, where inter-racial faculty, occasional white students, and frequent white visitors created a microcosm of the future. In the Center, racial barriers were gone and one got a feeling sometimes that this was not part of the Deep South. But for many years, that insulation which protected the University Center's island of integration also kept the city of Atlanta from feeling the resentment of Negro students against segregation. It was a comforting protection, but it also helped perpetuate the mystique by preventing contact. Thus, Spelman girls, more sheltered than women at other colleges and now the first to leave the island, began to cause little flurries of alarm, not only in the segregated world outside but in the sanctuary itself.

When those fourteen Spelman girls were arrested that first day of the Atlanta sit-ins, they were beginning the attack on the hallowed traditions of moderation, gentility, and abstinence from social struggle which had marked the college during its seventy-five years of existence. Of those fourteen, thirteen were from the Deep South, places like Bennettsville, South Carolina, Bainbridge, Georgia, and Ocala, Florida—the Faulknerian small towns of traditional Negro submissiveness.

The demonstrators, as the *Atlanta Constitution* noted, were marvelously disciplined and orderly. A Spelman honor student sat behind bars quietly reading C. S. Lewis's *The Screwtape Letters* while flashbulbs popped around her.

That was Marian Wright, now a graduate of Yale Law School and a civil rights lawyer. She once walked into our apartment on campus in the midst of the sit-ins carrying a notice she was about to post in her dormitory. Its heading combined perfectly the past and present of the Spelman girl. It read: "Young Ladies Who Can Picket, Please Sign Below."

A new spirit thus brought Spelman girls outside the wall into the community, in headlong attack on the racial mystique which depends so much on walls, physical and emotional. What was the source of this spirit? It seemed that something fundamental was at work, setting free for the first time the anger pent-up in generations of quiet, well-bred Negro college women, not only at Spelman College, but at Fisk, Bennett, Tougaloo, and other institutions throughout the South. The same warm currents which had been loosening the ice blocks of the status quo throughout the world also drifted into the South and mingled with local eddies of discontent. What has been called a global "revolution in expectations" arose here too in the hearts and minds of Southern Negroes.

Expanding international contacts reach even into

small Southern colleges. Marian Wright, from Bennettsville, South Carolina, had spent a year in Geneva as a
Merrill Scholar studying international relations and a
summer in Soviet Russia. The Atlanta student who
helped draft the Appeal, Roslyn Pope, had just returned from a year studying music in Paris. Under the
auspices of nationalist leader Tom Mboya, a small
group of young African women flew from Kenya to enroll at Spelman. The tame-sounding phrase "cultural exchange" has begun to have revolutionary political im-
plications.

In 1960 the advance guard of a long-term exchange
program—a handful of white students from Northern
colleges, soon visible in classrooms and dormitories—
came South and Spelman began to lose both its provincial air and its status as a segregated school. There was
a burgeoning of contact, both intellectual and social,
with students from the half-dozen white colleges in Atlanta. Young, liberal Southern whites began to join the
faculties of the Negro colleges.

The effects of change moved, though in diluted form,
from students to faculty and administrators. Many professors, who were distressed and critical when they first
learned their students were behind bars, later joined in
the applause of the Negro community and the nation at
large. Spelman's President Albert Manley, who inher-
ited the traditions of conservatism and moderation
when he took the helm ten years before, began to respond with cautious encouragement to the boldness of
his young women. At the college commencement exer-
cises in 1960, he startled the audience by departing
from the printed program and the parade of parting
platitudes. He delivered a vigorous statement of con-
gratulations to the senior class for breaking the "docile

generation" label with its sit-ins, demonstrations, and picketing.

But three years later, the excitement of the sit-ins over, Negro conservatism held fast to its power over Negro students straining to break away. At Spelman, student protest against antiquated rules was stifled, and punitive measures were taken against students and faculty members who spoke their minds. Teachers and students who refused to be contained by presidential edict began to leave the college. That dissident Negro students and white teachers should join in rebellion against a coalition of white and Negro administrators and trustees was in itself a thrust at the mystique of race.

When I first joined the Spelman faculty in the fall of 1956, a girl in my Western Civilization course spoke candidly and bitterly about her situation and that of her classmates. "When I was little," she said, "my mother told me: Remember, you've got two strikes against you; you're colored, and you're a woman. One more strike and you're out—so be careful." The student continued: "That's the trouble with these Spelman girls. They're careful. They hardly utter a peep. They do everything right, and obey the rules, and they'll be fine ladies some day. But I don't want to be that kind of a lady."

She was not alone in her feelings, because after the sit-in movement the Spelman girls were no longer obedient. Their rebellion continued—against white supremacy outside the college and against suppression of free thought within. Perhaps racism is a kind of shroud which, when removed, only enables us to grapple more directly with *other* problems of freedom and justice.

Negro leaders have played their part in maintaining the mystique of race by encouraging artificial behavior on the part of Negroes, presumably to make them more acceptable to whites. The day the buses were desegregated in Atlanta, a mass meeting was held at a large Negro church. Ostensibly, it was to celebrate, to announce the court decision, and to spread the word throughout the community that now people should ride wherever they pleased on the buses. Instead, to the annoyance of militant Negroes, a leaflet was passed out to those who crowded the church that evening. It said: "You will be notified when we will tell you to begin helping to desegregate the buses and trolleys, but until then be quiet but friendly; proud but not arrogant; happy but not noisy. Be sure you are neat and clean at all times." The advice was well-meant but the effect was to perpetuate, both for Negroes and whites, the ancient Southern notion that Negroes, like children, need to be told how to behave. Anyone who has been on Atlanta buses knows that Negroes are as quiet and as clean as the whites who sit on these same buses. This kind of leadership may help to explain why to this day many Negroes in Atlanta still sit only in the back of the bus.

The world-famous sociologist E. Franklin Frazier, a Negro, persistently criticized the Negro middle class, charging that its bourgeois manners and traditional religion were a cloak for intellectual sterility. This artifice, Frazier said, was borrowed from the white middle class, which was itself intellectually and culturally barren. The Negro should look to his own heritage, create his own future, free from the encumbrances created for him by white society. Frazier's bold exposition of this

view, *Bourgeoisie noir,* was published first in France
and then by an American publisher as *Black Bourgeoisie.*

When young, Frazier was run out of Atlanta in an atmosphere of near-violence for publishing a blistering
article on the White Southerner. In 1957, famous for
his studies of the Negro in America, he returned to lecture at Spelman College. Five hundred people jammed
the auditorium, standing in the aisles and in the hall-
way to hear him. His old Atlanta friends knew him as
an irascible, fearless man who refused to cater to the
white man's conception of what the Negro should be
like. He smoked cigars, drank whiskey, and used direct,
pungent language, almost in a calculated affront to
those Negroes, who, to match their white brethren, cul-
tivated the manners of the smart set and the vocabulary
of the pedant.

His lecture at Spelman was typically blunt. The Negro, Frazier told his predominantly Negro audience,
was not doing enough to take his place in the modern
world. Blighted by centuries of subjugation, never
taken seriously by the white man, and never taking
himself seriously enough, he had much to overcome,
and he'd better hurry. The failings of the Negro, he
emphasized, are not peculiar to him; they are the failings of human beings, neither to be concealed nor de-
rided, but to be removed by deliberate action. The poor
and uneducated Negro was no special phenomenon; he
was a peasant, like peasants everywhere in the world.
And it is characteristic of the peasant to see himself as
the helpless victim of fate. When peasants are asked
how many children they want, Frazier pointed out,
their response was the same in every country: "As many

as the Lord sends." The difference between a peasant
and a civilized person is that the civilized person "tries
to determine his own destiny."

Frazier denounced those Negro newspapers and magazines that create a world of "make-believe," in
which successful businessmen are the heroes. It is the
role of education, to smash through this world of make-
believe and give the Negro a realistic picture of himself
and of the world. "Most of our schools are finishing
schools for the Negro middle class," he told the audience that night, speaking from the platform of one of
those schools.

The wall between the races, the barrier between the
Negro and a full, good life, was maintained by false
values, including an overemphasis on religion. "I went
to compulsory chapel in college for four years," Frazier
said, "and heard nothing in those four years but sugary,
sentimental slop." He urged skepticism, criticism, a rational outlook on life.

He was not directing a special attack on Negroes;
even those offended by his acrid comments knew that he
issued them in a spirit of love for his own people. He
knew, and said often, that the faults of the Negro were
those of people everywhere. "We have never invented
any crimes or sins that white people hadn't already
perfected."

A student asked him why he had written *Black Bourgeoisie*. The audience laughed and applauded at his
response: "White people have bamboozled us. Preachers have bamboozled us. Teachers have bamboozled
us, and kept us all bamboozled. What we needed was
someone to debamboozle us!"

In Frazier's plea for the Negro to recognize his own

past, there may be an idea for all middle-class Americans to ponder. The American who was the object of so much admiration for visitors from Europe in the nineteenth century was the pioneer, the direct man, the man who worked with his hands. He was the man not yet removed from forest, from factory, from the soil, who had the honesty of the working man as opposed to the pretensions of Victorian, post-Metternich Europe with its combination of Habsburg aristocracy and new commercialism.

In the twentieth century, with the large American upper and middle classes hiding from public sight those below, the Negro is the most vivid remaining representative of this proletarian-peasant culture. The poverty and illiteracy which are part of this culture should not be romanticized, but there is, in lower-class life, a certain honesty which deserves to be retained. Perhaps the Negro is the last guardian of a moral reservoir from which the entire nation may some day drink.

If the Negro and the white are to encounter one another as friends, they need to be able to talk candidly and laugh openly at themselves and at one another. One caution is in order, perhaps. The white person who finds himself for the first time in a truly close relationship with a Negro sometimes tends, if he avoids patronization and syrupiness, to make a fetish of directness to the point where it turns on itself in a painful way. A white person may use the word "nigger" in conversation with a Negro friend without worrying, but if he uses it often, the suspicion will grow, and it will probably be well-founded, that there is in this very attempt to simulate naturalness an overconsciousness of race.

In my living-room one evening were two of my students, both very bright young men, one a Morehouse man from Atlanta, the other a white exchange student from the North who was spending a semester at Morehouse. They had been driving leisurely around town that afternoon. As they passed a pretty white girl on the street, the white student said: "Don't you look at her—she's mine—she's white!" They both laughed. But as they kept driving around, the white student made the same joke a second and a third time, and by then his friend began to be irritated. They discussed this frankly, sitting together that evening, and we all learned something from the incident. It is possible, the Zen followers say, to try too hard to be natural.

There is much talk about the New Negro. Every critical period has brought him forth. Certainly Frederick Douglass, Harriet Tubman, and the others in the abolitionist movement, certainly the Negro leaders of the Reconstruction period, were New Negroes. In the 1920's, the Harlem Renaissance brought a flowering of Negro literary activity centered on protest and epitomized in the 1928 volume edited by Alain Locke, *The New Negro.* So the current upsurge of Negro militancy is another flash of that same moral indignation piercing the American sky.

The New Negro makes a special contribution to the breaking down of racial barriers and the dissipation of racial mystery. He propels himself into the attention of the white; he demands to be known, to be recognized. Unlike the average Negro, who waits for the processes of change to bring him into contact with whites, to let them know him, the New Negro forces his way into the white consciousness, not arrogantly, but also not apologetically. He says: "Here I am, in all my wonder and failings, and I insist on being recognized as a human being. I want both my glories and my sins to be thrown into the acccount of the entire human mass, with no thought of race."

These past few years in the South have produced countless specimens of this New Negro, each unique in his own way. The most famous of these is Martin Luther King, Jr., but he has many lesser-known friends equally noteworthy. King himself is a perfect example of the blending of the old and the new, of traditional Negro religion and modern philosophical thought, of emotion and intellect, of folk tradition and twentieth century sophistication. More and more young Negro ministers are taking to the pulpit with messages of social protest, grounded in intellect and supported emotionally by the old Baptist songs.

One remarkable example of a minister devoted to social action is Professor Samuel Williams of Morehouse College, under whom King studied. A minister of the Friendship Baptist Church in Atlanta and a professor of philosophy as well, Sam Williams has been in the forefront of the protest movement in Atlanta for many years, and he unsparingly attacks not only weak-willed white politicians and conservative Negro leaders, but the church itself. "The church has never been a leader in social change, always a follower," he tells his audiences. "And we mustn't expect any more from the church except that it will, as it has in the past, sanctify that which is accomplished by others."

E. Franklin Frazier would have been delighted with Samuel Dubois Cook, a classmate of Martin Luther King, Jr., at Morehouse College, who became, the year

I arrived in Atlanta, chairman of the Department of Political Science at Atlanta University. Cook, huge in physique and in intellect, was born in Griffin, Georgia. He was a football star at Morehouse, received his doctorate from Ohio State University, and became a political theorist of the first rank. Cook combines the proletarian earthiness of the rural South with the intellectual vigor that Frazier was constantly urging young Negroes to attain. His achievements as a scholar, and his courage in defending freedom of inquiry against its attackers in both races, make him a leading representative of the New Negro.

Another is Carl Holman, writer and professor of humanities at Clark College. Young, lean, and very articulate, he was one of the pioneers of civil rights activity in Atlanta. His pamphlet, "A Second Look at Atlanta," provided most of the facts, and some of the passion, for the student movement. Holman was a founder of the *Atlanta Inquirer,* a militant Negro weekly born during the sit-in movement. The *Inquirer* now continues to set off little explosions to shake some of the smugness that grows almost as easily as dogwood in Atlanta.

There is a new Negro lawyer in the South today. The old type defended his Negro clients well, but he had a tendency to be a little humble before white judges and white prosecutors. When I first saw Donald Hollowell in action in federal court in Atlanta in 1956, I was aware of a new phenomenon. Hollowell, with a style of cross-examination that kept everyone in a state of wonder, behaved as if it were *his* courtroom, as much as the judge's, as much as the white attorney's. He questioned white witnesses with a vigor that one is not accustomed to see in Negro lawyers in the South. When a white educator, in a school desegregation suit, used the word "nigger" on the witness stand, Hollowell wheeled around and thrust his finger at the witness: "What did you say, sir?" The man, taken a little aback, responded with something closer to the acceptable.

It is an education in itself for a white judge, a white attorney, and white spectators, to see bright Negro lawyers in action. These new attorneys are coming out of the universities of the North and are moving into cities and small towns in the Deep South. C. B. King, Jr., finished law school and went back to his home town of Albany, Georgia, to practice. Trying his first case, he encountered the wrath of the sheriff, who had known him as a boy playing in the streets and was now astonished to see him up front in the courtroom. The sheriff demanded that he sit "where the niggers sit." King insisted on staying in his rightful place, and by now he is an established figure in Southwest Georgia.

The New Negroes are of all ages. They are too numerous to name. They are everywhere. A colleague told me of the students in an all-Negro state college in Georgia who were forced to listen to the address of a state official who kept using the word "Nigra." The first time he said it, the audience began to stamp their feet. The next time he said it, they stamped louder. Each time he used it, the noise was thunderous. His pronunciation of the word began to change with each sentence, and by the end of the speech, it almost sounded, with a great effort on the man's part, like "Negro."

For small towns in the Deep South to face this New Negro is not easy, and the initial impact is often a violent one. A 33-year-old Negro physician, Otis W.

Smith, sat in our home one evening in Atlanta. He told us that, eight days before, he had quickly packed a small suitcase, instructed his wife to pack the remainder of their possessions and to tell his patients to find help elsewhere, and departed from Fort Valley, Georgia, an agricultural town of 12,000 where he was the only Negro doctor. He had left under duress of the law. "Run out of town," he smiled. "It sounds like something out of an old Western movie."

Dr. Smith was born in Atlanta. Dark-skinned and strikingly handsome, Smith played football, basketball, and baseball for Morehouse. When he was finishing Meharry Medical School in Nashville, he accepted an offer from the Georgia Board of Regents to help pay for his last year in medical school, in return for a promise to spend fifteen months in a rural area in Georgia. Fort Valley, in Peach County, seemed a likely place. The last Negro doctor in town had died several years before, leaving Negroes there (60 per cent of the town's population) at the mercy of those humiliations that often accompany white doctor–colored patient relations in the Deep South: entrance through the side door, separate waiting rooms, and sometimes the question "Do you have the money?" before sick calls are made to the house.

Fort Valley is one of those pleasant little Georgia towns as yet unblighted by the smell of industrial plants. Smith made a down payment on a house, hung out his shingle, and in no time at all his office was full. Fort Valley State College for Negroes hired him as the institutional physician, and he spent several hours each day at the college infirmary.

When Dr. Smith showed up in the delivery room of

the Fort Valley hospital, for his first obstetrical stint in the town, the two white nurses there stared at him, then left the room, with the Negro woman in labor on the table. He delivered the baby with the aid of a Negro attendant.

One evening, while he was talking on the telephone to a patient who needed his help, a white woman cut in on the party line and demanded that he get off so that she could speak. He told her he was a doctor talking to a patient. She replied: "Get off the phone, nigger." It's hard to say what an old-style Negro doctor would have retorted, but young Dr. Smith said, according to the woman, something like: "Get off the phone yourself, you bitch."

He was arrested the next day, brought into court before his attorney even knew that the trial was going to take place, and sentenced to eight months on the chain gang for using obscene language to a white woman. In prison, facing the chain gang, he was offered release if he would leave town immediately. Smith decided to leave, and the next day the Negroes in Fort Valley were without their doctor. The first encounter of the Old South with the New Negro is painful, but it is the pain of birth.

In May of 1960, with the results of the sit-in arrests still inconclusive, about one thousand New Negroes— along with some New Whites—gathered on the Atlanta University campus to celebrate the anniversary of the 1954 Supreme Court decision. They planned to march downtown to place a wreath on the steps of the State Capitol. Governor Vandiver decided that the march and the proposed laying of the wreath consti- tuted a threat to the security of the state. He called out the state troopers, who circled the Capitol, in full fighting regalia, armed with guns, billy clubs, and tear gas. The students marched, a handful of faculty members with them.

A radio news reporter, following the line of march in his automobile, listened to the singing of the marchers and apparently mistook the New Negro for the Old One. He stuck his microphone in front of a woman in the line, a Spelman College teacher of literature, and urged: "Sing into the microphone, won't you?" She replied indignantly in her crisp, Oxford English: "I certainly will not!" The parade, deflected by police, ended up in the Wheat Street Baptist Church, singing, among other things, "That Old Ne-gro, He Ain't What He Used to Be."

In the summer of 1960, with the eighty-three sit-in arrests still waiting to come to trial, and no action on the demands enunciated in The Appeal, the students decided to begin work on the private lunch counters. Success had just been achieved, by a combination of pressure and negotiation, in several other Southern cities. Rich's, the South's largest department store and creditor to much of the population of Atlanta through its charge-plate system, was an obvious target: it had four eating places, ranging from a quick-snack lunch counter to the plush Magnolia Room.

The usual sit-in technique wasn't feasible at Rich's, where Negroes simply would not be admitted in the first place. And at Rich's most popular eating area, "The Bridge," there were no stools at the food counter, only tables and benches nearby. A new method was called for. On a pleasant June day, a little before noon, at the call of the student movement, my wife and I visited Rich's. Thumbing through records in the music department were two Negro students, John Gibson and Carolyn Long, but we exchanged no greetings. Exactly at eleven-thirty my wife and I went to the lunch counter up on "The Bridge," and each of us ordered two cups of coffee and two sandwiches. We brought them over to an empty table and sat down. Immediately, John and Carolyn walked over from a nearby section of the store, sat down with us, and we all began to have our coffee and sandwiches. At exactly the same moment, another foursome, at the other end of the eating area, was doing the same. We had arranged for two groups to move simultaneously into the opposite ends of the lunch area, because one man had been stationed by Rich's precisely for the purpose of heading off prospective Negro diners, and it would be impossible for him to deal with both groups at the same time.

"The man" came over to our table and, nervous, said that Negroes could not be served in that lunchroom. "That's all right," John Gibson said politely, "we don't need to be served. We've already got our food." The man asked us to leave. We remained. Other diners looked at us curiously from nearby tables. Rich's, at that time, did not want to gain unfavorable publicity by calling the police and arresting us. Instead, they began to close the lunch counter, remove the food, clean the coffee urns. Other shoppers kept coming up to the counter to ask for food, only to be turned away, disappointed. Clearly these other people were more concerned about their lunch than about the presence of Negroes in the same lunchroom. Finally, attendants began to pile all the benches on top of the other tables and dimmed the lights. Our fellow sit-inners joined us; Lon-

nie King and a few other people in the student movement sat down at our table, and the whole group chat-
ted in the semi-darkness, in the ghost of what an hour
before had been a bustling cafeteria. Then, our point
made, we left.

In the fall, with the student body back in the Atlanta
University Center, the assault on Rich's began in earnest. Hundreds of Atlantans, mostly Negro and some
whites, began turning in their charge-plates. Picketing
of the store became a regular thing. The students were
now well-organized, calling themselves the Committee
on Appeal for Human Rights. They were led by tough-
minded Lonnie King of Morehouse, whose driving per-
severence had kept the student movement alive through
a year of turmoil, and by Herschelle Sullivan, a bright,
gifted Spelman senior just returned from a year in Paris as a Merrill Scholar.

My family and I were away in Boston for that academic year, but we were kept in touch by telephone
calls and letters from Herschelle, who had been my
student. By February of 1961, the boycott was beginning to have an effect on the whole downtown area, but
particularly on Rich's. During the first week in February, department store sales in the central city area were
down 12 per cent from the year before. Several mer-
chants were ready to desegregate their lunch counters,
but they wanted Rich's, the most powerful concern in
the city, to take the lead. Rich's refused, saying they
wanted to make sure the school segregation controversy
was settled first. In January the General Assembly,
responding to the governor's plea, had paved the way
for Atlanta school desegregation, but still Rich's did not
act. Instead, the store closed its restaurants. Unable to

sit-in at Rich's, the students mapped a plan of action against some other lunch counters.

Organized like a guerrilla unit, with walkie-talkies, cruising cars, telephone stand-bys, and a huge body of willing students to draw from, the Committee began its sit-ins in early February at various Atlanta lunch counters. This time, to draw more public attention and dramatize the boycott, they chose not to accept bail. I received a telephone call one night in Boston from Herschelle, who told me that seventy-five students were in jail and refused to leave on bond. A few days later, a letter came from her. "To date there are 82 students in jail and tomorrow all hell should break loose as the ministers are going to sit-in and be arrested, if Captain Jenkins continues to cooperate with us." The reference to co-operation was ironic; in their jail-no-bail phase, the students were grateful to policemen who didn't hesitate to make arrests. I read in *The New York Times* on February 15 that eight ministers had been arrested and had joined the students in prison.

Negotiations finally brought a settlement, though not without conflict between the conservatives of the Negro community and the student leaders. An agreement was signed in March for desegregation of the lunch counters the following fall, and by November of 1961, the department-store and dime-store lunch counters, as well as a few of the best restaurants in the downtown area, were desegregated. It soon became a common sight to see Negroes dining at Stouffer's Restaurant. Although race-relations groups complained that not enough Negroes took advantage of the desegregated facilities, it was clear that, when they did, everything was peaceful.

My own relation to the student movement had been that of an observer, a friend, and an occasional participant. I had picketed supermarkets, sat-in at Rich's, gone with my students to desegregate the gallery of the legislature, picketed the State Capitol, and marched downtown in a mass parade. But I was arrested only once in Atlanta, and it had nothing to do with any of those actions. It is a story that has its own intrinsic interest, I believe. Essentially the incident reveals the traditional mystique of race consciousness that the South is just beginning to overcome: a mystique that expresses itself in the rage which inflames some white Southerners who see a white and a Negro together as friends, a rage which will fade as massive and equal contact becomes a fact in the Deep South.

It was in January of 1960, a rather cold, dark night. Driving off the campus, I stopped to give a lift to a student who was going in the same direction. It was a Spelman honor student, recently returned from a year in Paris. We talked, rode on. I parked the car and we were still chatting when powerful headlights swept through the car. A patrol car stopped near us. Two white policemen ordered us out of the car and into the back seat of theirs. "If you're arresting us, what is the charge?" I asked. The older patrolman turned to face us from the front seat. "You sittin' in a car with a nigger gal an' wantin' to know what's the charge?" We were taken to the police station and booked, charged with "disorderly conduct."

I told the sergeant behind the desk I wanted to make a telephone call. He said, "You'll get a chance to make it upstairs." I was put into a large cell with several men arrested for drunkenness and a young fellow who paced the floor despondently; there were rows of bunks with steel springs, no mattresses. I called to the guard and said I wanted to make a call. He pointed to a dilapidated-looking pay telephone inside the cell. I reached into my pocket. No dime. I had a dollar bill and called to the guard for change, but he said he couldn't change it. The young fellow nearby took a dime from his pocket and handed it to me. I dialed the number of Don Hollowell, the Negro civil-rights lawyer. Nothing happened; no dial tone; my dime was lost. The young fellow gave me another dime. I tried again. That dime was lost too. No one else had a dime. I waited.

After a while, I saw a Negro attendant pass outside the cell and got him to change my dollar for me. I called to the guard that the telephone was out of order. He came into the cell and looked at me with scorn. "Fella, don't you know how to make a phone call?" He lifted the wire beneath the telephone box. It was cut completely through. He lifted the two pieces and said, "You got to hold these wires together; that's how to make a phone call here."

Holding the wires with one hand, I finally reached Attorney Hollowell. He arrived soon (perhaps it was the first time those white guards had seen a Negro attorney), put up the money for the student and me to leave jail, and we drove back to the campus. A few days later, he managed to get the charges against us dropped. It was a Kafka-like episode, a relic perhaps for future historians.

In May of 1961, when I and my family were finishing our year in Cambridge, I received a letter from Herschelle Sullivan, which enclosed the front page of the *Atlanta Journal.* Across the entire top of the page was a headline: NEGRO LEADERS SUE IN U.S. COURT FOR COMPLETE CITY INTEGRATION. Near the headline, Herschelle had scrawled in pencil: "We've been graduated —we're no longer *student* leaders!" In a dramatic legal move, four of the student leaders, acting as their own attorneys, had filed suit against discrimination in every public facility in the city of Atlanta: parks, swimming pools, tennis courts, the municipal auditorium, the municipal courts, and everything else connected with the city. In their brief, the four young people called it "a suit to exhume much of the cancerous racial segregation that is festering within Atlanta." They filed it on May 17 to celebrate the 1954 Supreme Court decision of that date. At the moment, it seemed like a move mainly designed for public effect—but a year later, when the federal court got around to the suit, the injunction asked for in it was granted. It was the most sweeping legal victory for civil rights in Atlanta's history, and four students had done it on their own, as good an example of the New Negro in action as one could ask for.

It is commonly said that the white man cannot possibly know what it is like to be a Negro. I have argued earlier in this section that although no person can know *exactly* how any other individual feels, everyone can know *something* of the feelings of another, regardless of race or nationality or class, because all humans share the same range of human emotion. Segregation is a barrier to such knowledge, in both the North and the South. But writers like William Faulkner and Lillian Smith, by the power of their literary imagination, have managed to give white people a glimmer of what it must be like to be a Negro in the United States. Recently, John Howard Griffin in *Black Like Me* has done the same. It is incredible how many whites do not know, specifically, what Negroes experience in a segregated society. A man who is now an official in a race-relations organization in the Deep South told me that not until he was in his thirties did he learn for the first time, from a talk with a Negro political scientist, what it meant for a Negro to drive through the Deep South: the difficulty of finding a place to eat, getting a drink of water, using a bathroom, finding a place to sleep.

In the fall of 1962, some of my students wrote for me about their first encounters with racial discrimination. Their statements may serve as a vicarious contact with the life of millions of Negroes as it is every day.

A girl from Brunswick, Georgia, wrote: "I was in the 8th grade. There were four of us, my sister and my two brothers and myself, standing at one of the front windows of the local Dairy Queen, patiently waiting to be served. After about five minutes of standing, we were told to go to the side window. Upon approaching the side window we were told to always go around to the side window because it was the window for colored people. Some of my schoolmates and I would go to the Dairy Queen from time to time after that and purchase ice cream with our lunch money. I always led the way to the side window because I knew where it was. As I grew older, I found myself looking for a 'colored' sign everywhere."

An Atlanta student wrote about her experience on a bus: "As I sat down, the woman whom I sat beside immediately stormed out of her seat, trampling over my legs and feet, and cursing under her breath. Simultaneously, several other white passengers began to curse under their breaths. I was eighteen years of age at the time. Never had I seen people staring at me as if they hated me to the utmost degree. Never had I really experienced being directly rejected as though I were some poisonous, venomous creature."

A girl from Birmingham, Alabama, wrote: "I cannot remember a 'first encounter' with prejudice. It is something of which I have been aware for as long as I have been aware of myself."

Another student from Winter Park, Florida: "I was four years old when I encountered prejudice. I went to the family doctor with my mother, and upon our arrival at the doctor's office I made the mistake of sitting in the white reception room. The nurse immediately told my mother that we would have to go to the section reserved for Negroes."

"Every year there came to my southern bias city a state fair," wrote an Atlanta student. "Never before had I been told that 'You can't ride until these white children finish,' or 'You can't eat until we fix a place in the back for you.' "

Another student: "When I was about five years of age my grandmother would carry me to town. We had to ride the bus and I would always get on the bus and sit down in the front seat if it were vacant. After she paid our fare, she would get me by the hand and tell me to come and sit in the back with her."

A student from Durham, North Carolina: "A white teen-ager invited us to a youth forum at the church. But as we entered, the youth adviser stopped and told us that we were not welcome at that Church. She also said that the forum was not for us but for their youth and we should talk this over with 'our' God."

An honor student from Forsyth, Georgia, wrote: "I guess if you are from a small Georgia town, as I am, you can say that your first encounter with prejudice was the day you were born. Can you believe that my parents never got to see their infant twins alive because the only incubator in the hospital was on the 'white' side?"

When I put this question to the students in my class, I had forgotten that one member of the class was white, the first white girl to enroll as a regular student at Spelman College. Her reply to the question "What was your first encounter with prejudice" throws light both on the specific way in which the mind of the Southern white deals with the Negro and on the function of contact.

> Growing up in a small town in Kentucky, I was exposed on all sides to strong prejudice toward the Negro. Had I been asked how I felt about the problem, I would probably have quoted verbatim remarks about the "niggers" made by my grandparents.
>
> I experienced prejudice of my own in the summer of 1960. I was employed by a small research organization in Virginia just outside of Washington. I had been there three years when one morning, upon my arrival, I discovered a young Negro sitting behind the reception desk. I was at first shocked and then extremely troubled that the company would do this to me—a loyal and hardworking employee.

About ten o'clock I was called into the personnel office. As I sat waiting I tried to decide whether to turn in my resignation or hang on for a while. Surely they wouldn't keep her. It couldn't work! I would wait—keep out of her way—keep my friends away from the office—and it wouldn't last long.

"Miss. . . ., I've an assignment for you! Please spend the rest of the week at the reception desk with our Miss. . . . so that you can give her detailed instructions on operating the switchboard."

I was no longer confused or willing to compromise. I was enraged. The solution took place in my mind. "Yes . . . I'll train her." . . . By the time I got through "training" they would be more than pleased to see her go.

I crossed the hall and entered the reception room . . . the young girl stood and extended her hand. I don't know what happened at that moment—perhaps it didn't all happen then. I knew I wanted to help her. She stood erect and courageous; her eyes revealed question and fear; her words were warm and sincere.

She learned her job quickly and well. Before the end of the summer we were taking picnic lunches to the river's edge where I would listen as she told of her life as a Negro or read poetry in French. . . .

The Negro girl at that reception desk was Marian Wright, who had just graduated from Spelman College. And a year later, in the fall of 1961, the girl from Kentucky enrolled as the first white student at Spelman College.

Only occasionally—because we are so much involved in the serious battle for justice—do we stand off and look at this nation and the South from afar. When we do, we must conclude that the whole matter of race is more than evil, more than simply immoral; it is idiocy, the invention of a god gone mad, a playing out on an enormous stage of the supreme drama in the theater of the absurd. Perhaps humor, which recognizes the absurdity, is the most effective acid in dissolving the mystique of race. This is why Dick Gregory, the Negro comic, is such a serious commentator on our time. That is why, to the surprise of whites who have come prepared for intense earnestness, Negro leaders, in the midst of the most difficult campaigns, will use humor from the speakers' platform, and why Negro audiences will respond with uproarious laughter. I recall how surprised I was, at a bus desegregation rally in Atlanta, to hear the great Negro orator John Wesley Dobbs convulse his audience by telling them of the Negro window cleaner who fell from a sixth story building and swerved just before he hit the ground because a white woman was standing there.

The mood in which I have written thus far is one of hope, because I think too many people are discouraged by what they consider a mysterious and impenetrable problem. I have tried to show that, in spite of the feelings of the Southern white, he can be induced to change his behavior, overnight, by the skillful use of the hierarchy-of-value concept. I have suggested that his feelings of prejudice are not imponderable and ineradicable and that they can be dissolved, much faster than we realize, by massive and equal contact.

But with this hopefulness, useful in encouraging people to act, must go the recognition that all the progress made thus far in the United States is just the bare beginning of a necessary revolution in human conduct. Most of the Deep South (and much of the mid-South and a good part of the North), is still a social wasteland for the white, a jungle of cruelty and poverty for the Negro. What we have done so far in this last decade is like that first flickering of an electric light which immediately went out, but which signaled to its inventor, as he sat in total darkness, that it would work.

When the Wright Brothers flew an airplane for just 59 seconds, they knew the problem of flight was solved. Only in that sense can we be optimistic about the race question in America. It was clear after that flight that intense effort would be required to enable man to fly. The same is true for us in this instance. Time alone is a neutral container. It needs to be filled with action.

Such action will inevitably be initiated by Negroes, for there is no stopping them now. The response to these actions by the Southern white—and he is the same man in Atlanta as in Albany, in Georgia as in Mississippi, in desegregated Louisville as in segregated Jackson—depends on the leadership given in his own community, and by the national government.

The government of the United States has still not used its tremendous capacity for leadership in the South. With inevitable Negro initiative, with expected white wavering, such leadership is crucial. That is why the story of Albany, Georgia, told in the next part, is important.

PART THREE

Albany, Georgia:
Ghost in the Cage

Nowhere does the South envelop you so completely as in the Black Belt. All around Albany, Georgia, in nearby "Terrible Terrell" County and "Bad Baker" County—as in most of Mississippi, Alabama, South Carolina, Louisiana—the mystique of the South is overwhelming, stifling, depressing.

A nineteen-year-old boy, who came out of Terrell County to rest with us a few days in Atlanta, showed us the burn on his arm and blood on his shirt from the shotgun blasts that had grazed him and wounded another voter-registration worker a few nights before. He asked wryly: "Why is Hollywood still producing Westerns instead of Southerns?"

A week before, on the outskirts of Albany, Georgia, as I sat with another college student in a wild, black blaze of music in a Negro nightspot, he said to me between swallows of beer: "In Terrell, I always walk facing traffic. The other day a man in a truck tried to run me down."

The Southern mystique, under attack in the border states and the metropolitan centers like Atlanta, Louisville, and Nashville, finds its last refuge in the Black Belt country of the Deep South. There it crouches, an invisible beast in a darkened cage, while the government of the United States, like an uncertain circus guard, pokes with its stick and occasionally snaps its whip, but hesitates to enter the cage. Hearing, in the roar of the beast, the echo of the cannon fired at Bull Run and Fredericksburg, our national political leaders prowl warily around the cage, not realizing that the sounds they hear are only echoes, that the crouching figure in the corner, more ghost than substance, waits only for someone decisively to clang open the door, so it can flee.

With all its verbal adherence to equal rights, and its occasional spurts of action, our national government has paused too long, while too many have suffered, in deference to the man-made mystery of the rural, Black Belt South. It has left the Negro there at the mercy of violence, dispensed by officers of the law. The executive branch of government particularly, retreating before the mystique, has abrogated a responsibility which was written into the Constitution by the Founding Fathers, and underlined in blood by the Civil War: to enforce constitutional rights in every corner of the Union, with all the ingenuity and, if necessary, the power, at its command.

And the American citizenry, in turn, have created a mythology of their own about the role of the national government in the South. Based on the premise that its leaders are motivated primarily by moral considerations, liberals have expected too much, and radicals, seeing our moderate government as deliberately devilish, have expected too little. But no mysterious stirrings of moral passion will decide national policy on race. The government—like individuals—has a hierarchy of values, in which political self-interest is at the top.

Moral considerations have always waited for a chance congruence with political interest, so that the latter, at least briefly, might be eclipsed. These rare eclipses awaken awe, and self-delusion, in the liberal viewer. (Thus the Emancipation Proclamation, which was one of those, led us to underestimate the political factor in Lincoln's moral concern.) Our Negro citizens, sensing this, have set out to *create* self-interest for the government by mass demonstrations. Such demonstrations are intended to show Americans and the world the moral passion of long-silent Negroes, and also to reveal to national politicians the potential political power of twenty million neglected citizens.

The first of these mass demonstrations against local police power which have shaken the South and the nation these past few years took place in Albany, Georgia. In the actions of the principal figures in that drama —the Negroes, the whites, the police, and the executive branch of the United States government—there may be lessons for the future.

In December 1961, I received a telephone call at my home on the Spelman College campus from Dr. James Moss, an energetic young sociologist, a Negro, who was research director for the Southern Regional Council— an Atlanta organization which specializes in gathering data on race relations in the South. "You know there's trouble in Albany and we want a report on it. We'd like you to go down there for us. You see, we couldn't decide whether to send a white or a Negro, so we compromised." We both laughed, and I agreed to go.

. . .

Many Georgians call it All-benny. All around was cotton country and slave country before the Civil War, and Albany was a trading center, the seat of Dougherty County. W. E. B. DuBois, in *The Souls of Black Folk,* described the area:

> For a radius of a hundred miles about Albany stretched a great fertile land, luxuriant with forests of pine, oak, ash, hickory, and poplar, hot with the sun and damp with the rich black swampland; and here the cornerstone of the Cotton Kingdom was laid.

At the turn of the century, Albany was a placid little town. Blacks outnumbered whites, slavery was gone, and segregation was firmly in place.

Today, the city is a four-hour drive straight south from Atlanta, past scraggly cotton, clusters of Black Angus cattle, and beautiful brown fields of pecan trees. Wide-avenued and clean, it lies south of Kinchafoonee Creek, on the banks of the Flint River. It is a commercial center for Southwest Georgia, where corn, cattle, and pecans are traded, and it attracts tourists, new industry, and travelers heading toward Florida. "Tenth fastest booming city in the U.S.A.," the man at the Chamber of Commerce said proudly. "There's the rating—in black and white."

Albany always rated higher for whites than for blacks, and this is at the root of the mass demonstrations and mass arrests that shook that little city to its bones first in December 1961, then again the following summer. Negroes today make up 40 per cent of Albany's population (23,000 out of 56,000) and zero

per cent of its political officials. The entire machinery
of justice in the city and county becomes machinery for
injustice when Negroes are involved—for the judges,
juries, prosecuting attorneys, sheriffs, deputies, city police are all white.

Again and again the statement was made to me by
white people in Albany—in the office of a political
leader; in the anteroom of a businessman; in the living-
room of a middle-class family: "Albany has always
had good race relations . . . Our colored folks have
been satisfied . . . We have made considerable progress. . . ." In a nation with ten thousand history teachers, memories remain poor; the same statements were
made in Montgomery before the bus boycott, in Atlanta before the sit-ins, and all through the South in the
days of slavery.

Yet, the argument cannot be dismissed without meeting it, for it rests on certain facts: that the relations in
Albany were peaceful; that the Negro community
raised no shouts of dissatisfaction; that progress had
been made. Only when moved out of simple isolation
into the texture of life itself do these undisputed facts
become part of a much more complex vision of Negro
life.

In a market where social goods are unevenly dis-
tributed, peace must always be paid for. The price, paid
in the South by blacks and received by whites, began
in recent years to seem not quite right. And the mis-
taking of silence for satisfaction has often been the ruin
of a dominant group in the social order, for it usually
pays little attention until centuries of accumulated
grievances gather and explode. The white South has
been notably unequipped with the kind of social seis-

mograph that would detect the first faint tremors of unrest, and has been too far out of touch with Negroes
(the physical proximity of blacks and whites at work
in Albany and elsewhere is offset by the social distance
inherent in unequal status) to hear any but the loudest
noises. Thus, Southern whites were hurt and shocked
by the eruptions of the past few years.

In Albany, deep in the Black Belt, the shock of the
Negro demonstrations was particularly great. This was
so because white and Negro residents have starkly
different perceptions of the city in which they live. A
city political leader respected by many Negroes, who
was twice mayor of Albany and is a law partner of the
present mayor, could not believe, when I spoke to him,
that Albany Negroes were dissatisfied. James "Taxi"
Smith (a champion runner in college, he once got tired
in a cross-country race and took a cab the rest of the
way) said: "Outside agitators have caused all this
trouble. Those Freedom Riders are getting $100 a day.
Minimum! Some getting $200." Albany Negroes, he
said, "get as fair trials as white folks. Same crime, same
sentence." (On the other side of town, the story was
different. A Negro businessman whose independence
irritated the city fathers was fined $400 for a traffic of-
fense, someone pointed out.) As for juries, Negroes got
on the lists, Smith said. Had any Negroes actually served
on juries? "Well, I don't think it will work in this situation."

"Progress" occurred almost as frequently as "satisfaction" in the lexicon of white comments on race relations
in Albany. Like the confusion of peace with satisfaction,
and silence with consent, here was another failure to
understand the complexities of social change. The evi-

dence is strong that it is precisely *progress* which brings the clamor for *more* of the same. The American colonists on the eve of the Revolution, France under Louis XVI, Russia in the early twentieth century, India and some of the African territories in our time—all were making progress when the social fabric was burst by revolution. For progress creates *expectations,* and if the pace of this progress, no matter how swift compared with the past, does not match the ballooning of expectations, more drastic change is in order.

This century has created expectations for Negro Americans which cannot be satisfied by things like the air-conditioned segregated school, which was pointed out to me pridefully by the civic leaders of Albany. True, Albany Negroes live on clean and pleasant—if unpaved—streets, in a town where roses bloom in December, where there are no concrete skyscrapers or billowing smokestacks to mar the beauty of the surrounding countryside. White residents are friendly and helpful in personal contact. White lawyers have defended Negro clients. "A. T. Walden (Atlanta's venerated Negro attorney) would phone me from Atlanta and ask me to handle this case for a poor colored boy. And I'd do it." Ten years ago streets were paved in some Negro areas, the Negro football field was lighted, and a liaison committee kept contact with the Negro community. (When the committee wanted to go beyond the paving of streets, and started talking about hiring Negro policemen, it fell into disuse.) And then there is— it must be mentioned at least twice, to give a slight notion of how often it is mentioned by Albany's white leaders—the air-conditioned school.

To the Negro community however—and this was

one of the hardest things for whites in Albany to understand—all this was like improving the food inside a
prison; because all progress was within the framework
of a sharply segregated society. In the year 1961, a Negro arrived in Albany on the colored part of the bus,
entered a colored waiting room, drank from a colored
fountain, used a colored restroom, walked eight blocks
to find a restaurant which would feed him, and traveled
six miles to find a good Negro motel.

Once inside the city, the Negro avoided trouble, for
the courts were segregated, the jails were segregated,
and the judges, juries, sheriffs, deputies, and city police were all white. Tax forms for Negroes had a special
color. There were (and are) no Negroes in city or
county government; but there were well-educated, cultured, and competent Negroes in Albany, who could
have moved immediately into the highest municipal offices and brought credit to the community. Negroes got
jobs in Albany only after color had narrowed the field
to a slit. "If I can do a job as good as a white man, why
shouldn't I have it?" a Negro porter asked me as we
stood on the steps of the white church where he was
employed.

To see the situation on the most elemental level, a
white man would have had to recognize somehow that
no Negro in downtown Albany could stoop to a water
fountain before making sure it was labeled "colored."
On a level both more abstract and more heartfelt,
whites would have needed to comprehend, even dimly,
the attack on his dignity felt by every Negro adult male
who is called "boy." There is a basic hurt attached to
being an American Negro—both North and South—
which cannot be conveyed by a cold list of specific
grievances. In Albany before the demonstrations, there

was no way for fair-minded white people to know these things. There was contact, but it was superficial. There was exchange of words, but not of feelings.

Although communications between the races inside that little city were crude, between Albany Negroes and the outside world they were as advanced as modern science could make them—through radio, television, air travel, national newspapers and magazines. There were the mails, no longer closed as in Abolitionist days to the arguments for racial equality. Besides this, there was the fact that several thousands of Albany's population were attached to Air Force or Marine Corps units in the area: integrated units. Young Albany Negroes had gone to college in other parts of the country. In the spring of 1960, the only college in the city, Albany State College for Negroes, became aware of the winds blowing from Atlanta, Nashville, and Greensboro.

Early in 1961, the century-long quiescence of Albany Negroes began to break. Perhaps it had been shaken by the sit-ins, freedom rides, and boycotts which had been successful elsewhere in the South, perhaps vaguely stirred by the rise of colored peoples in Africa and Asia, or, more likely, by a combination of factors too complex for easy categorization.

In February, a group of Negro leaders in Albany had presented the city commissioners with a request to initiate the desegregation of certain municipal facilities. The *Albany Herald,* the city's only daily, answered for the City Commission and flatly rejected the request. About the same time, sporadic incidents occurred on the Albany State College campus, where marauding whites in automobiles threw eggs, fired shots, and even tried to run down a Negro student.

It was against this background of local unrest, frustration, and developing action that the Atlanta-based Student Non-Violent Coordinating Committee (SNCC, familiarly known as SNICK), sent a team into Albany in September 1961, to register Negro voters. SNICK was born out of the sit-in struggles of 1960 and was staffed by a small group of former college students who had experienced jailings and beatings in the sit-ins and Freedom Rides. They set up an office in a run-down little building two blocks from the Shiloh Baptist Church, began to register Negro voters in the city, and through their enthusiasm and energy acted as a catalyst to a community which had already begun to stir.

On November 1, 1961, in direct response to the Freedom Rides of that summer, the Interstate Commerce Commission handed down its ruling that all train and bus facilities used for interstate commerce were to be desegregated and were to show signs announcing this. SNICK, whose members had gone to jail through the summer to force this ruling, was ready to test it in the segregated terminals of Albany on the very first day of its existence.

Charles Sherrod and Cordell Reagan, two veterans of the Freedom Rides who were now in the SNICK Albany office, rode down to Albany from Atlanta on the Trailways bus. Sitting a few seats away was a white college girl from Memphis named Salynn McCollum, a friend of SNICK who was prepared to witness the test of the ICC ruling. When they arrived in Albany, they caught sight of police waiting at the terminal, and decided to postpone the test until later that day. To evade the police, Salynn raced through the streets and back alleys of Albany to find the home of Irene Wright, one of the city's leading militants. Then, in a makeshift disguise, she slipped out of the house, got to the bus terminal, and stationed herself in a position to watch nine young Negroes, who had been mobilized quickly by Sherrod and Reagan, ordered out of the white waiting-room. SNICK then notified the Department of Justice.

That was the first test of whether the national government would enforce the ICC ruling, and it failed the test. Nothing came of the complaint. On November 17, SNICK, the local NAACP, the colored ministerial alliance, and other Negro groups in Albany got together to form the Albany Movement and elected local osteopath Dr. W. G. Anderson as president and retired railroader Marion Page as secretary. They expressed their determination to attack discrimination in these key areas: bus and train stations, libraries, parks, hospitals, buses, juries, public and private employment, and treatment by the police. One of the leaders of the Movement said about its birth: "The kids were going to do it anyway . . . they were holding their own mass meetings and making plans . . . we didn't want them to have to do it alone."

The second test of the ICC ruling came on November 22. That morning, three members of the Youth Council of the NAACP in Albany were arrested by Chief of Police Pritchett for returning to the Trailways Terminal lunchroom after he had ordered them out. And in the afternoon, two Albany State students, tiny, soft-voiced Bertha Gober of Atlanta, and Blanton Hall, who came from Athens, Georgia, were arrested for going into the white waiting-room. (They became the first of forty students expelled by Albany State College for participating in the Movement.) With those two incidents, the Department of Justice failed its second and third tests. It did nothing to enforce the ICC ruling.

The fourth test, on Sunday, December 10, was the most dramatic. Again, the Department of Justice failed, and by that failure ignited the spark of racial conflict that exploded in Albany the week before Christmas.

That Sunday, the Student Non-Violent Coordinating Committee, in consultation with the Negro community of Albany, decided to try again the much-broken ICC ruling. Eight young people, Negro and white, of both sexes, took the Central of Georgia Railroad from Atlanta to Albany, sat together in the "white" car, ignored a conductor's demand that they move, and continued that way on to Albany. Several hundred Albany Negroes gathered at the Union Railway Terminal to meet them.

It was about 3:30 in the afternoon, a quiet time in Albany, with little traffic and few whites near the station. A. C. Searles, the Negro editor of the *Southwest Georgian,* a regional weekly, watched the scene. Waiting also were police and newspaper reporters. The eight riders got off the train, went into the "white" waiting-room, and sat down. Police Chief Pritchett told them to get out. They left, accompanied by Charles Jones of SNICK and Bertha Gober, and walked to cars outside the terminal which were waiting to take them into town. Searles heard Police Chief Pritchett call out: "I told you to get off the street. You are all under arrest." Some of the ten were already getting into cars. All of them were now ordered into the paddy wagon, along with Willie Mae Jones, an Albany student who was in the crowd watching. The eleven were charged with obstructing traffic, disorderly conduct, and failure to obey an officer, with bond set at $200.

Police Chief Pritchett's version, as reported in the press, was: "I told the demonstrators to move away from the terminal three times; then we called the paddy wagon and I gave the order to arrest them. We will not stand for these troublemakers coming into our city for the sole purpose of disturbing the peace and quiet of the city of Albany."

Editor Searles interpreted the incident as follows: "There was no traffic, no disturbance, no one moving. The students had made the trip to Albany desegregated without incident. Things had gone so smoothly I think it infuriated the chief." Months later, Mayor Asa D. Kelley of Albany said the arrests had been a mistake.

With the eleven in jail, the Albany Movement went into action. The next seven days saw a series of mass meetings by the Negro community and marches downtown by over a thousand Albany Negroes, singing and praying, asking freedom for the arrested students and, as one woman said after her release from prison, "to get our rights." The silence of a century was being broken.

When the trial of the eleven was to take place at the city courthouse on Tuesday, December 12, over 400 Negro high school and college students marched downtown to protest, singing as they went by the courthouse. Police cars with loudspeakers ordered them to disperse, but they continued to walk. Then they were herded into a fifteen-foot-wide alley running alongside City Hall, where they waited in a driving rain for two hours as police booked them one by one on the same charges leveled against the Freedom Riders. That night at a mass meeting at the Shiloh Baptist Church the audience sang hymns and heard speeches by leaders of the Albany Movement. Many of the jailed were being released on bond, but 153 remained crammed into the Dougherty County jail and early the next morning were transferred to jails in "Terrible Terrell," "Bad Baker," and other neighboring counties.

On Wednesday, three different demonstrations took place. As court convened in the morning, about 70 Negroes marched downtown and knelt on the sidewalk in front of City Hall to pray. Their spokesman, Slater King, member of a distinguished Negro family in Albany, was arrested and sentenced to five days for contempt of court. In the early evening, 300 Negroes made one slow circuit around City Hall, returned to the Shiloh Baptist Church, re-formed, marched back to City Hall, and were arrested on charges of unlawful assembly, parading without a permit, and unlawfully congregating on the sidewalk. Chief of Police Pritchett told newsmen: "We can't tolerate the NAACP or the SNCC or any other nigger organization to take over this town with mass demonstrations."

On Friday night, Martin Luther King, Jr., invited by the Albany Movement Executive Committee, arrived from Atlanta with Rev. Ralph Abernathy and spoke to a packed prayer meeting at the Shiloh Baptist Church. King told the audience of over a thousand: "Don't stop now. Keep moving, Don't get weary. We will wear them down with our capacity to suffer." Ruby Hurley, Southeastern Regional Director of the NAACP, spoke too. "There are only two languages the white politicians and the power structure understand. One is the power of the almighty dollar bill. When those cash registers are not ringing they understand what you're talking about. They also understand the ballot." And the Albany Movement's chairman, Dr. W. G. Anderson, said: "Be here at 7 o'clock in the morning. Eat a good breakfast. Wear warm clothes and wear your walking shoes."

On Saturday evening, December 16, came the climax of the demonstrations and mass arrests as Martin Luther King, Jr., and W. G. Anderson led 250 hymn-singing men, women, and youngsters down Jackson Street toward the county courthouse. Police Chief Pritchett stopped them two blocks from the City Hall and asked King if he had a parade permit. King said, "We are simply going to pray at City Hall." Pritchett ordered the entire group arrested for parading without a permit.

They were moved into the alley near the City Hall. Police cars rushed up to seal off the back of the alley, white onlookers were cleared off the sidewalks by police loudspeakers, and the Negroes were led one by one into the police station and booked. A Southern white student from Brunswick, Georgia, had marched with them and was also jailed. King, Abernathy, and Anderson were sent to Sumter County jail in Americus. Now the total arrested stood at 737, with over 400 people still in jail, many of them farmed out to prisons in nearby counties. Late Saturday night, sound tracks moved through the city calling military personnel back to the Air Force and Marine Corps bases. Police closed bars and liquor stores.

Negotiations had been fitfully under way, and they resumed Monday morning. The Albany Movement was represented by C. B. King; Attorney Donald L. Hollowell of Atlanta, the state's leading lawyer in civil rights cases; and Marion Page, acting as chairman of the Albany Movement now that Anderson was in jail. These three conferred with the Police Chief, Mayor, and City Attorney at City Hall. Verbal agreement was reached on these terms: the acceptance by the city of desegregation in train and bus facilities; the release of all the demonstrators from jail on the signing of simple property bonds, with the exception of the original Freedom Riders of December 10 (eight of whom were still in jail); the calling off of further demonstrations; and a promise by the city to hear the Negro community's case at the first business meeting of the new City Commission.

I arrived in Albany the day after the agreement, as hundreds of Negro men and women were coming out of the jails. At the Shiloh Baptist Church, almost the first person I encountered was SNICK worker Charles Sherrod, just out of Terrell County jail, his voice low-pitched, penetrating, as he told about the Terrell jail and Sheriff Zeke Mathews. When the group was locked up, the Sheriff announced: "There'll be no damn singin' and no damn prayin' in my jail." Sherrod told him: "We may be in jail, but we're still human beings and still Christians," and the Sheriff hit him in the face. They took him into another room, and another officer hit him.

In a corner of Shiloh Baptist Church, demonstrators who had been fired were lined up to see Ella Baker. She is a middle-aged, handsome Negro woman, with a voice that belongs on the stage, who has moved silently through all the protest movements in the South, doing the things that the famous men don't have time to do. She had been there hour after hour without a break, noting names, occupations, addresses, immediate money needs. The people waiting on the bench talked to me about their jail experiences.

Fifty-one women had been sent to the Lee County stockade. There was no place to sleep, just wet and dirty mattresses in the cell.

Eula Jackson spent four days in "Bad Baker" county jail: "Peas and grits are what they gave us. They would put it on the floor and kick it into the cell. I didn't eat for four days."

Another woman: "We were 88 in one room from Saturday night to Monday night, with 20 steel bunks and no mattresses . . . Sheriff took us to Camilla. On the bus he told us: 'We don't have no singin', no prayin', and no handclappin' here.' "

A man arrested Saturday night: "No one put a hand on me, but I feel like I been beaten. When you sleep on steel and concrete you are automatically sore. I'm a trailer driver, on the job a year, came back to work this morning, found I got no job. They told me: 'You a Freedom Marcher.' "

Another man: "Forty-two of us in a cell for 12 in the city jail. Then we were put in a bullpen, 60 men, 16 beds, all standin' up on one another. The food? Oh bad, man!"

A young married woman, senior at Albany State College, left two children with her mother and demonstrated Wednesday evening. She slept on an iron cot in the city jail and got sick. From Wednesday to Friday she ate nothing. Slater King, in the same prison, tried to slip his food to her through a hole in the door, but a guard came along and hit him in the back.

One of the women had worked a year at a cleaning establishment. Thirty dollars a week, $28.10 net. Six days a week, twelve hours a day. When she was forced to work until 10 P.M. one night and got no extra pay, she left her job, got another. Now, with her arrest, that job was gone too.

It wasn't the prison conditions that hurt these people deep inside, but the reason for it all. The young woman from Albany State said: "I didn't expect to go to jail for kneeling and praying at City Hall."

The Shiloh Baptist Church was packed that night, as it had been every night since the demonstrations began. Freedom songs, a few speeches, spirited reactions from the audience. In the middle of the meeting, the young white girl from Georgia who had been arrested with the original riders from Atlanta walked down the aisle to the microphone. She had been released from jail a few minutes before and was out of breath. She spoke briefly in her soft Southern accent: "First time I've ever been in jail. It's a funny mixed-up feeling to hate being in a dirty place—but to be glad you're there for a good reason . . . Hope you'll keep going."

Eight of those original Freedom Riders whose arrest had started the mass demonstrations were still in jail, and I tried to see them the next day. One of them was Lenore Taitt, my student at Spelman, who had acted together with my wife in *The King and I,* a delightful girl, far from the sober agitator—a happy Freedom Rider, of unquenchable spirit. I walked downtown to the Dougherty County Courthouse. The sun was warm, though it was December; roses were blooming on the walk leading into the courthouse. Far in the back I could see the jail—a small stone building surrounded by a barbed-wire fence. Inside the courthouse, Chief Deputy Sheriff Lamar Stewart, tall, husky, unfriendly, puzzled a minute over my request: "You want to see a nigger gal?"

"I want to see one of my students."

"You want to see a nigger gal."

"I want to see one of my students."

It went on like this for a while.

"Why don't you sleep with her?"

"I just want to see her."

"She's one o' them Freedom Riders ain't she?"

"That's right."

"Can't no one see any prisoners."

"No one? How about their parents—husbands—wives?"

He shook his head. "No one but a preacher or a lawyer."

"No way I can talk to her?"

"You can holler through the fence like every one else does."

I walked across the yard to the barbed-wire fence that encircled the jailhouse. I pressed against the fence and shouted Lenore's name at a thick steel mesh window twenty-five feet beyond. It was impossible to see through. I heard noises and then a cry of recognition, the reaction unmistakably Lenore Taitt's, but her voice was incredibly hoarse.

"What's the matter with your voice Lenore?"

"I lost it yelling all Saturday night. Twenty-six women who'd been in the parade Saturday night and got arrested came in with us. We were already full, six beds for six people. They brought in four mattresses for the twenty-six. For five nights we slept three on one of these narrow cots. One of the women got sick Saturday night. They had taken her glasses away and her head

hurt. She cried, just stood around and cried. I kept yelling out of the window for help, but no one came. All
night long I kept calling and no one came. Sunday
morning, a trusty brought food and I asked him to get
the jailer. He came back and said the jailer wouldn't
come. My voice has been like this ever since." (Two
months later, in Atlanta, Lenore's voice was still abnormal; then gradually, it came back.)

Later that afternoon, some of us waited near the fence
while Attorney C. B. King was in the courthouse paying
the bond on the Freedom Riders; then they came out,
blinking, into the sunlight: Lenore Taitt, Jim Forman,
(SNICK's veteran executive secretary), Norma Collins (secretary in the SNICK Atlanta office), Per
Laursen (a young writer from Denmark), and Bob
Zellner, Alabama-born, one of SNICK's white field
secretaries. We all went to the Harlem Drug Store in
Albany's Negro section, a gathering place for people
in the Movement, and they had their first post-prison
meal. Then to Irene Asbury Wright and her airman-
husband Vic Wright, whose home had become a haven
for young freedom-fighters.

Bob Zellner told us that when he went into the
county jail, the sheriff noted with suspicion that he had
two paperback books with him. One was *Tropic of
Cancer,* which the sheriff glanced at and returned to
Zellner. The other was *Strange Fruit* by Lillian Smith,
and the cover suggested that it dealt with a romance
between a Negro girl and a white boy. The sheriff took
it away, saying, "This is obscene!"

The settlement that brought a peaceful Christmas to
Albany gave few concessions to the Negro movement,
and a front-page story in the New York *Herald Trib-*

une called it "one of the most stunning defeats" in the career of Dr. Martin Luther King, Jr.

For the city to agree to the desegregation of the terminal facilities was belated recognition of what became law on November 1. The release of the demonstrators simply restored the situation before the arrests. Trials and jail sentences still hung over everyone at the discretion of the police chief. The City Commission promised to listen, but not necessarily to act.

No long-term assessment of the Albany actions could be based on what was or was not conceded at the moment of settlement. This was a Deep South city, with a hundred-year history of Negro silence and white complacency which had now been shattered for all time. Anyone who sat in the Shiloh Baptist Church at that prayer meeting after the settlement could tell that expectations had been raised which would not be stilled without a change in the social patterns of the city. "Albany will never be the same," Attorney Donald Hollowell told the crowd that night, and he was right. The call for a boycott at that meeting came not from the platform, but from the audience, and was echoed by a dozen men and women who stood up amid shouted approval and called, with the passion of people who have tasted prison, for Negroes to stay away from the downtown stores.

Analysts coolly added up concessions on both sides and came out with a mathematical sum that signified defeat. But the Negroes of Albany had no such feeling. A Negro porter on the steps of an Albany church said to me: "No, we're just beginning. Just beginning." And Irene Wright said, as we were talking over the situation: "Anybody who thinks this town is going to settle back and be the same as it was, has got to be deaf, blind, and dumb."

That truce of December 1961 did not take much time to fall apart. On Friday, January 12, an eighteen-year-old Negro girl named Ola Mae Quarterman, a former student at Albany State College, sat down in a front seat of an Albany city bus. The driver left his seat, poked his finger near her face, and the conversation went something like this: "Don't you know where you're supposed to sit?" Her reply: "I paid my damn twenty cents and I can sit where I want." He called a policeman and she was arrested and jailed. The reason for the arrest, Police Chief Pritchett said, was that she had used vulgar language ("damn").

"I used the word 'damn' in regard to my twenty cents, not to the driver," Miss Quarterman later stated at a federal court hearing, but the distinction seemed lost on the court. At that hearing, the city attorney tried to establish that she was arrested for using vulgar language, rather than for sitting in the front of the bus. It was all part of an elaborate judicial game now being played in Southern courtrooms in which everyone pretends that the race of the arrested person was the farthest thing from the policeman's mind, and tries to invent interesting new charges for the arrest.

But Ola Mae Quarterman did not want to play. When the city attorney asked, "You weren't tried for sitting where you were sitting, were you?" she replied quietly, "That's what they said," and then repeated more loudly for the benefit of the court, *"That's what they said."*

Miss Quarterman was found guilty in city court of using "obscene" language, and a boycott by Negroes of the city bus system, already underway, was intensified.

In less than three weeks the company, dependent for much of its revenue on Negro customers, halted operations. White businessmen, fearful of the effect on their trade, met with representatives of the Albany Movement and the bus company to get the buses back into operation, and reached what was probably the first important desegregation agreement in Albany history: that the buses would resume on an integrated basis and would accept applications from Negroes seeking jobs as drivers.

But obstinacy on both sides got in the way. The City Commission, with Mayor Asa D. Kelley the lone dissenter among its seven members, refused to give written assurance that it would not interfere with bus integration (there was a municipal ordinance requiring bus segregation). And then the Albany Movement decided not to accept an agreement on the buses without some sort of assurance on other requests. The bus company tried to run again but finally quit for good and disposed of its equipment. Public transportation came to an end that March in Albany and has never returned.

Two days before the Ola Mae Quarterman incident, several groups of Negro students who tried to get cards at the white Carnegie Library had been turned away, directed to the Negro library, and questioned by police. One week after the arrest of Miss Quarterman, SNCC workers Charles Jones and Charles Sherrod, sitting in the Trailways lunchroom, were arrested by city policemen for "loitering." Again, the color of their skin was avoided. "We don't allow people to go in there and just make it their home." Chief Pritchett said.

Everybody had been waiting for Tuesday, January 23, when, by the verbal agreement of December, the

City Commission would hear spokesmen for the Albany Movement. That evening Anderson and Page presented to the Commission a petition with requests for the desegregation of various city facilities. They were told to await a reply. One week later the Commission issued a statement denying all the requests of the petition: "The demand for privileges will scarcely be heard, wherever and whenever voiced, unless . . . arrogance, lawlessness, and irresponsibility subside." Negro leaders could "earn acceptance for their people," the statement said, "by encouraging the improvement of their moral and ethical standards."

Mayor Kelley, supported by Mayor pro tem Buford Collins, dissented from the Commission's response, approved by the other five members. He said that it evaded the basic issue: "In my judgment the city of Albany has got to recognize that it has a problem and cannot solve that problem by sticking its head in the sand and ignoring that problem. No solution can be reached unless there are lines of communication."

In March, the trial of the original Freedom Riders jailed by Chief Pritchett on December 10 began in the county court. When Charles Sherrod entered the courtroom that morning, he walked down front to the "white" section and was immediately knocked to the floor by Chief Deputy Lamar Stewart, who pulled him back to the rear of the courtroom. Bob Zellner and two other white defendants, Tom Hayden and Per Laursen, as well as Tom's wife, Sandra Hayden—a tall, attractive blonde girl from Texas—sat down next to Sherrod in the rear. Deputies pounced on them and dragged them out of the courtroom. One deputy pulled Mrs. Hayden over a row of seats and pushed her through a revolving door outside. Judge Carl E. Crow watched all of this and then told newsmen: "The officers were enforcing a rule of the court."

In April, more trouble took place. Dr. Anderson, Slater King, Emanuel Jackson, and Elizah Harris, four leaders of the Albany Movement, were found guilty of "disorderly conduct." They had been picketing a downtown store as part of the general Negro boycott of stores which did not hire Negro employees. Also, Charles Jones, Cordell Reagan, and two others were sentenced to sixty days on public works gangs for refusing to leave a drugstore lunch counter at which they had sat and requested service. And 26 more people were arrested in lunch-counter sit-ins.

About the same time, a Negro café-operator in Albany named Walter Harris was shot to death by a policeman who claimed Harris had attacked him with a knife while resisting arrest. Perhaps there was a need now to make up for the silence that had followed previous slayings of Negroes by police officers for "resisting arrest." Perhaps there was a recollection of the killing in late 1961 of a Negro man by a sheriff in Baker County under similar circumstances. Or perhaps the Negro community was still conscious of the imprisonment since July 1960 of Charles Ware, who was shot repeatedly through the neck by officers of Baker County for "resisting arrest." At any rate, 29 adults and teenagers appeared in front of City Hall after the Harris shooting, to protest. Refusing to disperse, they were arrested, and when some youngsters lay down on the sidewalk in a show of passive resistance they were picked up and carried into police headquarters.

Meanwhile, Martin Luther King, Jr., and Ralph

Abernathy had been called back to Albany from Atlanta to stand trial for leading that parade in December. The defense attorneys, led by Donald Hollowell of Atlanta, argued that the arrests were based on the desire to maintain segregation, that they violated the First Amendment rights of free speech and assembly, as well as the Fourteenth Amendment right to equal protection of the laws. But the city said race was not an issue in the arrests at all; the Chief of Police was merely enforcing a statute that required a permit for parades. When Hollowell asked Pritchett how a "parade" was defined, the Chief answered that there was no definition. "Then it's anything you want to make it?" Hollowell asked. "In my opinion, yes," was the reply.

King and Abernathy were found guilty and sentenced by Recorders Court in Albany on July 10, 1962, to 45 days or $178 for leading the December 16 demonstrations. Hollowell asked Judge Durden for the legal citations on which his decision was based. The judge said he didn't have any, but that it was based on "general research of the law."

The defendants chose to go to jail, and excitement rose to a high pitch not only in Albany but throughout the nation. Senator Joseph Clark of Pennsylvania told the Senate the convictions were evidence "that there are still, unfortunately, areas of our country in which the Constitution of the United States, as represented by the Fourteenth Amendment, is not in effect." That evening, when police cars showed up near the two Negro churches where mass rallies were taking place, bricks and rocks were thrown at them, and Chief Pritchett put his whole force on a standby alert.

The following day, Wednesday, 12 men, 9 women,

and 11 teen-agers of both sexes—32 Negroes in all—
began to walk to town. Two blocks away from the
downtown area they were stopped by Chief Pritchett
and arrested. They marched to the city jail, two squads
of police behind them, singing "We Shall Overcome"
while curious whites watched quietly. That night, with
hundreds of Negroes gathered outside the Shiloh Baptist Church, bricks and bottles were thrown at the police across the street.

The jailing of King, as no other event in the history
of Albany's troubles, sent Washington officialdom into
a flurry of activity. President Kennedy asked Attorney
General Kennedy for a report on the Albany situation.
Robert Kennedy and Burke Marshall, head of the Civil
Rights Division of the Department of Justice, made a
number of telephone calls to Albany. Marshall assured
Mrs. King in Atlanta that the Department of Justice (according to *The New York Times*) "would use whatever
influence it could to obtain his release."

The next morning, King and Abernathy were released. How this happened has never been made
clear. According to Chief Pritchett's report, an un-
identified, well-dressed Negro man showed up at City
Hall and paid the fines. The two ministers, who were
anxious to stay in jail as a sign of the sacrifice required
in the struggle, reluctantly left. Dr. Abernathy told a
mass meeting that night: "I've been thrown out of lots
of places in my day, but never before have I been
thrown out of jail."

Dr. King now attempted to open negotiations with
the City Commission on a desegregation timetable, but
all overtures were rebuffed. A battery of high-powered
legal minds assembled in Albany to plan legal action

against segregation: William Kunstler, of the American
Civil Liberties Union, Clarence Jones and Constance
Motley of the NAACP, Donald Hollowell of Atlanta,
and C. B. King of Albany. The Albany Movement began a series of moves to lay the groundwork for court
cases.

On Tuesday, July 17, twenty-five Negro students
showed up at the Carnegie Library to ask for library
cards and books; they were turned away. The next day,
forty teen-agers staged sit-ins, in teams of eight, at five
different lunch counters downtown, which were immediately closed. Reporter Fred Powledge noted in the
Atlanta Journal that in at least two cases, the students
were asked to leave not by managers, but by policemen. At the Trailways Bus Station, a fifteen-year-old
Negro boy tried to enter the restaurant and was refused. "I asked him why," the boy related. "He said it
was because I was a Negro—he didn't say Negro
though. He said nigger. You know."

That Wednesday afternoon, eighty young Negroes
tried to use the athletic facilities of Tift Park and were
ordered to leave by Detective Captain Ed Friend and a
group of other officers. On Thursday, seven Negro
youngsters were jailed in a lunch-counter sit-in, and
fifty others were turned away from the white picnic
area of Tift Park. On Friday, more groups were turned
away at lunch counters and ordered away from a swimming pool by the assistant chief of police.

With a mass prayer meeting scheduled by the Albany Movement for City Hall on Saturday afternoon,
Mayor Kelley and Albany's City Attorney, Henry
Rawls, flew to Atlanta to confer with Governor Vandiver's legal staff, then to Columbus to see Federal Dis-

trict Judge J. Robert Elliott. Elliott, longtime associate of the Talmadges in Georgia politics and a public supporter of segregation, had just been appointed to his post by President Kennedy. At midnight on Friday, July 20, Elliott issued an omnibus injunction that barred "unlawful picketing, congregating or marching in the streets . . . participating in any boycott in restraint of trade" and, in fact, "any act designed to provoke breaches of the peace." The injunction was to hold until July 30 when a hearing on a similar permanent order would take place.

With the temporary restraining order in effect, the planned Saturday afternoon demonstration did not take place, but in the evening a group of 160 persons, young and old, began to walk from Shiloh Baptist Church toward City Hall, and were arrested under orders of Chief Pritchett. The Trailways lunchroom was also closed that day when Negroes tried to enter. But the *Atlanta Journal* reported: "The same attendant was seen admitting white people to the lunchroom."

More than 100 of the Saturday marchers were under 18, many of them 13 and 14 years old, and they were sent to Camilla in nearby Mitchell County. "They call it a juvenile detention place," one youngster said. "But it's just an old jailhouse." Sixty-four were put in a cell designed for 12 children, 52 others in a cell designed for eight.

On Monday, July 23, about 5:30 P.M., Mrs. Slater King, wife of the Albany Movement's vice-president, and in her sixth month of pregnancy, drove to Camilla with a group of other Negro women to take food to the daughter of a friend. She had her three children along and was carrying one of them, a three year old. Two deputies ordered the group away from the outer fence around the jail. "All you niggers get away from the fence," one of them demanded. The women began to move away, Mrs. King walking slowly to her car. One of the deputies pointed her out, cursed her, and said if she did not hurry, she would be arrested. She turned and said, "If you want to arrest, go ahead." The next thing she knew she was kicked and knocked to the ground. An officer hit her twice on the side of her head and she lost consciousness. She revived in about ten minutes and, since no one else in her car could drive, managed to drive back to Albany. Months later, Mrs. Slater King lost her baby.

Monday evening, after a rally at the Mt. Zion Baptist Church, a group of seven, led by Mennonite minister Vincent Harding, stopped in front of City Hall to pray. (Vincent Harding is a Negro with striking intellect and courage, and a strong faith that love and non-violent action can creatively join whites and Negroes in a new brotherhood.) They had been troubled by the beating of Mrs. Slater King. Chief Pritchett ordered them to move on, but they stayed in place and were arrested.

The next night, when forty people were also arrested in a march toward City Hall, what had started as a non-violent parade (reported *Atlanta Constitution* correspondent Bill Shipp) "degenerated into an angry, catcalling crowd" and an estimated 2,000 Negro youngsters gathered at the edge of the Negro area. Dozens of rocks and pop bottles flew out of the crowd at the police and injured one state trooper.

Earlier the same day, Tuesday, July 24, Judge Elbert P. Tuttle of the Fifth Circuit Court of Appeals had set aside Judge Elliott's temporary restraining order. He pointed to a fatal flaw in its constitutional argument: the Fourteenth Amendment provision on "equal protection of the laws" was not designed to protect the state against individuals, as the temporary injunction suggested, but was intended to protect individuals against state action. In other legal moves that day the lawyers for the Albany Movement filed two suits against the city of Albany: one to desegregate the city's public facilities; the other to prevent the police from interfering with peaceful demonstrations.

That evening, in the face of a request by Negro leaders to appear at its regular Tuesday meeting, the City Commission postponed the meeting. A newspaperman pointed out: "The City Commission steadfastly refused to confer with any Negro leaders about racial problems during a seven month intermission in mass racial demonstrations."

Wednesday was quiet, having been declared a "day of penance" by Dr. King and Dr. Anderson for the violence of the previous evening. Thursday was uneventful, too, but on Friday at 2:15 P.M., King and Abernathy led a group of ten to City Hall to try once again to talk with the City Commission. Chief Pritchett asked them to leave, pointed to a nearby group of newspapermen and photographers, and said, "You can see you're causing a disturbance." As Abernathy began to pray, Pritchett ordered the group arrested. Two hours later, a group of 18 youngsters left Shiloh Baptist Church for City Hall. They knelt on the sidewalk to pray, refused to move when the Chief ordered them to do so, and were arrested.

One of the young people arrested was a white

SNICK field worker from Cincinnati named William Hansen; he was promptly put into the white section of Dougherty County jail. Putting him into the cell, a deputy sheriff said to a trusty: "This is one of those guys who came down here to straighten us out." The trusty replied: "Well, I'll straighten him out." As Hansen sat on the cell floor reading a newspaper, he was attacked and beaten into unconsciousness. His jaw was broken, his lip was split, and a number of ribs were broken. He was then transferred to the city jail.

Late that afternoon, Saturday, July 28, Attorney C. B. King, brother of Slater King, visited Sheriff Cull Campbell of Dougherty County to check on the condition of Hansen. Seeing King in his office, the Sheriff said: "Nigger, haven't I told you to wait outside?" King turned to say something. The Sheriff pulled a walking stick out of a basket (a sign on the basket says they are made by the blind and sell for 50¢ to courthouse visitors) and brought it down with all his force on King's head. The attorney staggered from the office, blood streaming down his face and onto his clothes, and made his way across the street to Chief Pritchett, who called for medical aid.

New York Times reporter Claude Sitton quoted Sheriff Campbell as saying, "He didn't get out so Goddammit, I put him out." Sitton also noted in his story that "Chief Pritchett had more than 160 city, county and state law enforcement officers standing by to prevent violence." Pritchett had just arrested 28 Negroes for praying and singing for 15 minutes in front of City Hall. He called the beating of King "very regrettable."

After I arrived in Albany a month later on my second visit, I went to see Sheriff Campbell. The basket of

walking sticks was in the hall. The Sheriff invited me
into his office and said: "You're not with the goddam
niggers, are you?" I thought it better not to reply. Instead, I asked him about the affair of Attorney King.
He stared at me. "Yeh, I knocked hell out of the son-
of-a-bitch, and I'll do it again. I wanted to let him know
. . . I'm a white man and he's a damn nigger."

During that first week in August 1962, thirty persons, including one white woman from New York, were
arrested as they prayed in front of City Hall. An integrated group of five was arrested while trying to get
service at the Holiday Inn restaurant. The total of arrests since the start of the December demonstrations
now passed 1,100.

All that week and into the middle of the next, the city
and the Albany Movement argued before Judge Elliott
in Federal District Court on the city's petition for a permanent restraining order on demonstrations. According
to a UPI dispatch in the *Washington Post,* Chief Pritchett supported the request for such an order by testify-
ing that "racial tensions have reached a boiling point."
Two days before that testimony, the *Atlanta Constitution* reported that he had said: "People go about their
normal business. This city is nowhere close to an explosive point." A sophisticated knowledge of the laws of
physics probably could explain how the city had reached
a boiling point but was nowhere close to an explosive
point.

At the close of the hearing on Tuesday, August 7, the
Department of Justice, which had received dozens of
telegrams and a number of delegations, all asking action on behalf of Albany Negroes, filed a friend-of-the-
court brief in support of the Albany Movement's re-

quest to deny the injunction against demonstrations, noting that the city, because of its failure to desegregate public facilities, did not come into court "with clean hands." Judge Elliott reserved decision in the case. By now C. B. King, Abernathy, Anderson, and Slater King had been in jail two weeks, and they were released on Friday, August 10.

On Saturday, Negro individuals tried to enter the library and parks, which were immediately padlocked. Negroes also tried to attend services at white churches on Sunday, August 12, and were admitted to a Catholic and an Episcopal Church, but were turned away from a Baptist and a Methodist Church. On Tuesday, two persons were arrested for picketing a Negro theater whose white owner refused to admit two white persons, other Negroes were turned away from the snack bar at Phoebe Putney Hospital, and a white couple and six Negroes were arrested for attempting to use a bowling alley.

Among the youngsters at the bowling alley was sixteen-year-old Shirley Gaines, who had spent time in jail in Camilla back in April when she protested the killing of Walter Harris by police. Arrested at the bowling alley, she sat on the steps waiting for the paddy wagon to park nearby. As she waited, she later told me, two policemen threw her dress over her head, held her by the legs, dragged her down the stone steps to the bottom, and left her lying there. A man came along and kicked her in the side, and when she cried out a policeman standing nearby said, "Nigger, you can holler louder than that," then dragged her into the paddy wagon. With her back hurt, she lay on the floor inside City Hall. A man kept opening a swinging door near her, hit-ting her head each time. As she kept crying out, a policeman dashed water in her face to quiet her, and another called, "Holler, nigger."

A policeman then carried her, meanwhile kicking her with his knee, into the paddy wagon again, pushed her on the floor, and took her to Putney Hospital. But when the examiner found she couldn't rise since her back still hurt, she was taken to a city doctor. The doctor shone a light on her back, announced he found no injury, and said: "There ain't nothing wrong with that nigger. She got a good kickin'." She spent a day in city jail, then was examined by Dr. Anderson, who found her back bruised and scarred.

On Wednesday, August 15, the City Commission finally met a Negro committee face to face. Secretary Page of the Albany Movement read a petition that asked four questions of the city: 1. Would it abide by the ICC ruling on bus and train terminals? 2. Would it refund cash bonds on those arrested and accept tax receipts? 3. Would it refrain from interfering with desegregation in city buses if they would operate again? 4. Would it desist from interfering with peaceful protest? Mayor Kelley responded by saying that these matters were under consideration in federal court, that the decision of the court would be obeyed, and the meeting adjourned.

After the meeting, the Mayor told newsmen (according to a dispatch in the *Atlanta Journal*) that "he did not believe the city would take any action on the Negro requests." A mass meeting of 1,000 Negroes that evening heard Martin Luther King, Jr., and Page denounce the Commission's refusal to negotiate, and they heard Anderson announce that voter registration and the downtown boycott would continue, as well as other activities designed to budge the rigid stance of the city officials.

With Labor Day coming, 75 Protestant ministers, Catholic laymen, and Jewish rabbis drove down to Albany from the North to register their support for Albany Negroes. Praying in front of City Hall, they were arrested by Chief Pritchett, and sent off to various county jails, where they stayed for periods of two days to a week, a number of them fasting the whole period. Before arresting them, Chief Pritchett said: "You have come to aid and abet the law violators of this city and county. If you come as law violators, you will be treated as such. Go back to your homes. Clear your own cities of sin and lawlessness."

I drove down to Albany from Atlanta the last week in August, again on assignment from the Southern Regional Council to do a report. One of the first things I did was to visit Dougherty County jail, this time shouting at the windows on the white side, to talk to one of the ministers, a Yale Divinity School graduate named Bob Forsberg, whom I had met a year before. (He and his wife work in an inter-racial slum area in New Haven, living the social gospel more directly perhaps than any of the prophets of that gospel had foreseen.) The jailer came to the fence: "Yeah, those fellas are here. I wouldn't call them ministers. Nothin' like the ministers I know."

"How's the food?" I asked Bob. A silly question.

"We're fasting."

"What do you need?"

"Some books, a comb."

I bought a comb and some paperbacks across the

street and delivered them through a trusty who came to the barbed-wire fence. Then I went around to the Negro side to find Cordell Reagan, an eighteen-year-old SNCC veteran of many Southern jails. Cordell was up on the second story and I shouted for him to hear me. He'd been in jail sixteen days now, and he was depressed. "I need to get out of here. Real bad." I told him I would talk to C. B. King about rushing it. His bail money was on its way, but King was all involved in the federal court trial. With so many people in jail, with so much work to do, it was easy for individuals to be forgotten temporarily, which meant an extra day or two in that miserable hole. Cordell couldn't talk for long; he was standing up on a sink in order to reach the window to shout through the screen and across the courtyard to me. He wanted to tell me about his fellow prisoners, who'd been in there longer and needed help. Cordell had been arrested while sitting on a car fender watching two youngsters picket a segregated theater. The police had picked him up for "contributing to the delinquency of minors." Cordell shouted through the window: "Here I am, eighteen years old, contributing to the delinquency of minors!"

At the church that night at a prayer meeting, we listened to some of the Northern ministers just out of jail. A young rabbi came up to the rostrum. With intense feeling, he spoke of the Biblical injunction to treat strangers as brothers, spoke of himself and the other ministers as such strangers, who came to Albany. He quoted again and again from the Old Testament, and the crowd responded with "Yes! . . . Yes! . . . That's right!" as if he were one of their own Baptist hellraisers. Later, after a chicken dinner for the ministers in the church basement, they prepared for their return trip north. Outside the church, in a darkness punctured by faint lights from the battered frame houses of Negroes living across the street, with the motors of the bus throbbing in the background, people drifted over from all directions, gathered around the strangers and sang Freedom Songs, one after another, with intensity and love. It was an eerie, poignant scene.

I sat in federal court the next day as Judge Elliott began hearings on three cases: the city request for an injunction against demonstrations; the Movement's request for desegregation of city facilities; and the Movement's petition for non-interference with peaceful protests. (The trial was completed in late September. In February 1963, Judge Elliott announced that he had ruled against the Movement's requests on desegregation and non-interference.)

After the hearing I drove out into Lee County, where the night before the homes of some Negroes active in voter registration had been fired into from automobiles. As we stood on the porch of his house on the road going east from Leesburg, Negro farmer James Agnew showed me the burn on his son's leg, which had been grazed by a bullet as he lay sleeping on the couch. Farther on into the country was the farm of James Mays, whose house had been splattered with bullets. He pointed to where one bullet had ripped through a window sill, inches away from the body of a little girl who lay asleep on her bed.

After Lee County, Albany seemed a haven. I stopped off at the Harlem Drug Store before going on to the evening prayer meeting, and someone called to me. It was a dark-haired, good-looking white fellow, unshaven, weary-looking, in a tee shirt and jeans. I didn't recognize him until he told me where we had met. Six months before, at a conference of Northern students for civil rights, I had met this student from Trinity College. His name was Ralph Allen and at the conference he had seemed just one of many other neatly dressed youngsters interested in "the Negro problem." It was six months later, and here he was, just in from Terrell County where he'd been spending the last few months registering voters.

That evening, we went with Cordell Reagan, just out of jail, to relax and talk at the Parachute, a canvas-covered, music-and-beer place on the outskirts of town. Ralph Allen talked, over the dance music, about his experiences in Terrell County—the beatings, the disappointments, the beginnings of hope. A local political figure, now out of office, had once described Terrell County to an investigator from the Civil Rights Commission as "a feudalistic system." It was not an exaggeration.

In Terrell and the other Black Belt counties around Albany, the smell of slavery still lingers. Terrell and Lee Counties are north of Albany. To the south is Baker County. It was in Bad Baker, in 1943, that a Negro mechanic named Bobby Hall, while handcuffed, was beaten to death with a metal blackjack by Sheriff Claude M. Screws and two other officers. Federal prosecution of Screws, which would have resulted in one year in jail, failed on a subtle point of law. It was not clear, said the Supreme Court, that there was "intent" on the part of Screws to deprive Bobby Hall of his constitutional rights! In 1958 Screws was elected to the General Assembly of Georgia.

Terrell County has a long history of brutality against

Negroes. In 1958, a Negro named James Brazier was beaten to death by local police. The circumstances are described in the Commission on Civil Rights' 1961 volume, *Justice*. A local grand jury failed to indict. A year after this incident, Brazier's widow was told by Terrell County's Sheriff Zeke T. Mathews: "I ought to slap your damn brains out. A nigger like you I feel like slapping them out . . . I'm gonna carry the South's orders out like it oughta be done."

Former Mayor James Griggs Raines of Dawson has said: "In my opinion, the Sheriff, Mathews, is unfit and has violated the Civil Rights Acts. I've seen him beat a pregnant Negro woman. He's unfit to hold office. You can quote me."

Mathews himself has observed to a *Washington Post* reporter: "You know, Cap . . . there's nothing like fear to keep niggers in line." Sheriff Mathews is still Sheriff of Terrell County. A civil suit against him and the police officer who beat James Brazier was thrown out by a local jury in early 1963.

In Terrell County, Negroes are a majority of the population, but for a Negro to try to vote there has always required supreme courage. In 1960, out of a population of 8,209 Negroes, 51 were registered voters. Of the 4,533 whites, 2,894 were registered. The first suit filed by the Justice Department under the Civil Rights Act of 1957 was against the Board of Registrars in Terrell County; it resulted in a 1960 injunction forbidding discrimination. But the most powerful factors operating against Negro registration still exist in Terrell County: the threat of economic reprisals, an atmosphere of intimidation and repression, a history of brutality, the reluctance of the national government to curb the local police. The Civil Rights Acts may entitle the Negro to equal treatment inside the Registration office, but in the Black Belt, his problem is to *get there.*

Before the first wave of demonstrations began in Albany, SNCC field secretaries Charles Sherrod and Cordell Reagan, in November 1961, began a campaign to register Negro voters in Terrell County. They stayed at the home of Mrs. Carolyn Daniel, who operates a beauty salon in Dawson. Soon, police cars began prowling around the Daniel home. In early 1962, Sherrod, while visiting another SNCC worker who had been jailed on a traffic violation, was put in jail for "disorderly conduct." Sherrod bitterly criticized "the slow progress of the U. S. Justice Department in following through on complaints of brutality, intimidation, and harassment aimed at Terrell County Negroes."

At the start of the summer, the tiny SNCC group that was registering voters in Terrell County was joined by Ralph Allen. On July 4, while he and Joseph Pitts, an Albany student, were talking to some Dawson Negroes about voter registration, a white man struck Pitts on the head with a cane and slapped Allen. They complained to the Sheriff and were referred to Chief of Police W. B. Cherry of Dawson, who was involved in the Brazier killing. Cherry referred them to the Sheriff. Wanting to swear out a warrant against their assailant to prevent future attacks, they went to the home of Justice of the Peace Daniel English, who ran out and shouted to Pitts: "Get off my porch, nigger." Again, the SNCC office in Atlanta pleaded for action from the Justice Department.

On Saturday, July 21, Ralph Allen was walking down Railroad Street in Dawson when a truck tried to run him down. The driver jumped out and said: "You came here to show our niggers how to vote. I should kill you." Allen put his hands behind his back in the customary SNCC posture of non-violent response. The man hit him on the side of the head. He put his hands behind his back again. The man knocked him to the ground and began to kick him. Two others came along; one put his foot on Allen's throat, the other kicked him in the side. One drew a knife and said: "Should we kill him now?" But they finally let him go. The FBI in Albany dutifully copied down for their records what had happened.

The following Wednesday, July 25, a remarkable voter-registration meeting took place at the Mount Olive Baptist Church in Sasser, a rural hamlet in Terrell County. The meeting was reported vividly to the nation by Claude Sitton of *The New York Times,* Pat Watters of the *Atlanta Journal,* and Bill Shipp of the *Atlanta Constitution.* The forty persons at the meeting were mostly Negroes from the area. Also attending were SNCC workers Charles Sherrod, Charles Jones, Ralph Allen, and Penelope Patch, a nineteen-year-old Swarthmore college student. As Sherrod was reading from the Scriptures, thirteen white men, led by Sheriff Mathews, entered the church. Sheriff Mathews began questioning people, took names, warned Allen to leave the county, told the group it would not be to their interest to continue the meeting, and said to reporters: "We are a little fed up with this voter registration business . . . we want our colored people to live like they've been living for the last hundred years—peaceful and happy." When the meeting was over, a deputy sheriff said to one Negro leaving the church: "I know you. We're going to get some of you." Before going to the Sasser meeting, one of the newsmen had invited the FBI along, but they declined.

On Sunday, July 29, Ralph Allen and Charles Sherrod were arrested by Sheriff Zeke Mathews while accompanying Negroes to the voter-registration office. They spent five days in jail before being released on bond. When Allen asked what was the charge against them, he was told: "Investigation, vagrancy, and all that crap." Reporter Bill Shipp of the *Atlanta Constitution* wrote: "Terrell County Sheriff Zeke T. Mathews refused to let reporters see the warrant on which Sherrod and Allen were arrested. He also refused to show them the docket where the cases had been booked."

Perhaps spurred finally by the July 25 incident at Sasser, the Department of Justice on August 13 asked the U. S. District Court to prohibit law enforcement officials from intimidating prospective voters in Terrell County and to halt prosecution of Sherrod and Allen for their recent arrest. Judge Elliott refused to grant an immediate temporary injunction and said there was no evidence of immediate danger to the civil rights of those involved.

Two days later, a church that was used as a voter-registration center in neighboring Lee County burned to the ground. (On October 3, the FBI arrested two men, who were charged with setting the fire.) Two weeks later, in another night shooting incident, the homes of four Negro families active in voter registration were riddled by bullets, while children slept inside. On September 5, a SNCC registration worker was wounded by a shotgun blast in Dawson. And that week, the same Mount Olive Church in Sasser which had been the scene of Sheriff Mathews's invasion in July was burned to the ground. As of early 1964, Judge Elliott, apparently unconvinced that constitutional rights were in danger, still had not issued an injunction.

Who is responsible for the atmosphere of brutality which pervades Albany, Georgia, and its surrounding Black Belt counties? I don't mean, who is to blame for the long *history* of injustice in that area; for historians it is of scholarly interest, for others it is an empty exercise, to fix the responsibility for past sins. I am talking of responsibility for their *continuance*. When I speak of "blame," the intent is not to gain emotional satisfaction at finding a culprit, but to try to locate a focal point for constructive action in the future.

On whom will the pressure of indignation bring the maximum in results? The Negro? The white citizen of Albany? The local politicos and their power structure? The chief of police? Of all the forces in the Albany situation, it is the government of the United States that maintains the widest gap between verbal declaration and action, between potential and performance. The Negroes of Albany have strained to the limits of their capacity to endure pain and rebuff. The white community has behaved in accord with its untouched hierarchy of values. The chief of police has acted like something more than a chief of police; he has moved into a power vacuum and taken charge of the city of Albany. Only the national government has not lived up to its moral pretensions. And, in surrendering to the local police, it has not lived up to the Constitution of the United States.

Before the processes of social change through non-

violent pressure can work in the Black Belt as they
have begun to work in places like Atlanta, the stone
wall of police power must be broken. This police power
has herded Negroes into prisons in Albany, subdued
them with water hoses in Birmingham, left them open
to murder in Mississippi. It has prevented them from
voting, arrested them for distributing leaflets, crushed
their attempts at picketing, put them in jail for assem-
bling in protest for a redress of grievances. It has, in
other words, nullified the words of the First Amendment and the Fourteenth Amendment in a large part
of the Deep South. And the only force capable of dis-
mantling—without violence—this wall of police power,
is the United States government. So far it has shown no
such desire. This was first revealed in Albany.

Albany's white people are not different from the vast
majority of the white people in Atlanta and Memphis
and Louisville. They are—like Albany's Negroes—
mostly hardworking, quiet, peaceful people. An elderly
white couple, whose daughter I had met in Atlanta, invited me to tea and showed in their questions that basic
humanity deep in all Southerners, and of course in all
people, which will make race relations in the South
warm and noble once artificial obstacles are removed.

At no time during that first week of demonstrations
in December 1961, nor during the earlier incidents connected with the Trailways Terminal, were there any
mobs or angry crowds or voiced threats. One white man
sang "Dixie" near Negro demonstrators, and once
when a crowd gathered at the Trailways Terminal, a
few mutterings of hostility were heard. But signs of
deep tension were observed by no one, white or Negro,
to whom I spoke and who had been on the scene. *The*

New York Times reported in the midst of the trouble: "There were no indications that the 30,000 white residents of Albany were greatly aroused over the dispute."

Where whites did appear at the scene of the demonstrations, the chief motivation seemed to be curiosity. "What were the white people doing when you were marching?" I asked a Negro man. "Nothing but reckless eyeballin'," he said, and then smiled. "That's what I call it—reckless eyeballin'. Just curiosity."

When three Negroes were arrested trying to attend services at the First Baptist Church on August 19, 1962, the church's pastor, Rev. Brooks Ramsey, said: "This is Christ's church and I can't build any walls around it that Christ did not build." This should not be considered evidence of strong liberal sentiment among whites in Albany, but it does indicate that a bold man of stature in the community may dissent from prevailing opinion without suffering immediate reprisal.

All of this is to suggest that the white population of the city would respond to a leadership which moderately and quietly arranged for compromise agreements with the Negro population. But the city officials, thus far not encouraged to base their actions on the segregationist but passive white majority, have listened instead to an extremist minority. That minority is perhaps represented best by two symbols: James Gray, publisher of the town's only daily newspaper, the *Albany Herald,* which regularly prints racist statements of hate; and the sheriff who snatched a button from the lapel of one of the demonstrators, threw it to the ground, and stamped on it. The button read: "We Believe in Human Dignity."

The white population hangs on the edge of compliance. The local white leadership rests on the edge of compromise. The national government remains uncertainly at the foot of the cliff. And from down there, the policeman standing guard above appears as a giant.

Police Chief Pritchett was hailed in newspapers all over the country for preventing violence in Albany. An *Atlanta Constitution* reporter did a piece on Pritchett in which he did not conceal his admiration. A reporter for the New York *Herald Tribune* said Pritchett "brought to Albany a standard of professional achievement that would be difficult to emulate in a situation so made to order for violence. . . ."

Pritchett earned this praise by simply putting into prison every man, woman, and child who dared protest in any way the infringement of rights guaranteed to them by the Constitution. His glorification in the press may indicate that Americans have been led to a distorted view of the rights of citizens and the duties of police officers in a democratic state. Is it not the function of police officers to defend the rights of citizens against anyone who would prevent them from exercising those rights? The praise of Pritchett was a measure of the extent to which the purveyors of violence in Montgomery, Birmingham, McComb, Oxford, and elsewhere succeeded in their function: they have managed to lower the settlement terms for race crises in the South, so that the prevention of violence is sufficient as evidence of successful police action. Thus, the requirement of positive protection of equal rights is waived.

The pattern of arrests in Albany is quite clear: the police kept a peace which had not been broken, and with no signs that it was about to be broken, by putting into prison over 700 men, women, and children who were exercising basic American rights to assemble peacefully and to petition the government for a redress of grievances.

The pattern started on November 1, 1961—the day that the ICC order against discrimination in terminals took effect—when the Albany police ordered two Negroes out of the bus station in a situation where there was no crowd, no threat, no indication of either violence or tension. Three weeks later, November 22, 1961, again with no sign of disturbance, three Negroes were sitting quietly in the Trailways Terminal restaurant waiting to get the food they had ordered, when the police ordered them out. They left, returned, and were arrested. The same afternoon, two more students were arrested for using the white waiting-room. On December 10, the eight Freedom Riders were arrested—again with no signs of imminent trouble—as they were entering automobiles about to leave the scene. The mass demonstrations that followed resulted in the arrests of more than 700 people for walking downtown to the vicinity of City Hall. They were singing and praying, and the whites standing nearby were only staring in curiosity. In the midst of the marches, an Associated Press newspaperman reported from Albany: "White residents of this city have shown little close-range interest in the incidents." Here is how the pattern continued through the first eight months of 1962:

Students asking for library cards: questioned by police.
Girl sitting in front of the bus: arrested.
Two young men in the Trailways restaurant: arrested.

Four men picketing a store downtown: arrested.

Thirty young people trying to get service at lunch counters: arrested.

Ten people picketing stores: arrested.

Five people picketing: arrested.

Thirty-two people on way to City Hall: arrested.

One white and two Negroes in front of City Hall: arrested.

Group trying to use Tift Park: ordered out by police.

Students trying to get service at drug stores: ordered out by police.

Seven sitting at a lunch counter: arrested.

Eight students trying to use a swimming pool: ordered away.

One hundred and fifty people on way to City Hall: arrested.

Seven people praying in front of City Hall: arrested.

Ten people praying at City Hall: arrested.

Eighteen people praying at City Hall: arrested.

Sixteen people praying at City Hall: arrested.

Fourteen people praying at Carnegie Library: arrested.

Six singing at City Hall: arrested.

Nineteen praying at City Hall: arrested.

Five asking service at Holiday Inn restaurant: arrested.

Eight trying to use bowling alley: arrested.

Two students picketing theater: arrested.

Three Negroes seeking to attend church service: arrested.

Seventy-five ministers praying at City Hall: arrested.

There was no balancing in Albany between the rights of free speech and assembly and the police powers of the city. There was no consideration of imminent disturbance, or impending violence, no concern with what is the prevailing judicial rule for determining the limits of free speech—the existence of a "clear and present danger." Chief Pritchett has run the city of Albany in the silent, sure manner of an efficient police state.

True, Chief Pritchett did not torture or blackjack his prisoners. But is that enough to meet the standards of American freedom? Pritchett arrested more than 1,000 people for praying, singing, marching, or picketing. He did not make a single move toward arrest when Sheriff Campbell, just across the street, bludgeoned C. B. King and the attorney staggered, still bleeding, into Pritchett's office.

A report by the Georgia Council on Human Relations said: "The City Commission of Albany has officially given to the Chief of Police the power to be its spokesman in dealing with the Negroes. The Judge constantly refers to 'The Chief.' 'The Chief and I decided' . . . 'The Chief told me' . . . 'The Chief will set the date.' So not only does the influence of 'the Chief' extend over the City Fathers, but it also permeates the Court itself. As long as this condition remains, there can be no healthy, democratic government in Albany. There may be no large-scale violence, but there is little chance for the growth of justice and truth."

Chief Pritchett has not engaged in the worst forms of police brutality. But it is an evil thing for a policeman to deprive an entire community of human beings of their liberties. In an incident reported last summer by journalist Murray Kempton, a tiny boy showed up in the line of Negroes being booked at Albany's City Hall

after a protest parade. "How old are you?" Chief Pritchett asked.

"Nine," the boy replied.

"What is your name?" the Chief queried.

"Freedom, freedom," was the response.

The Chief said: "Go home, freedom."

The late President John F. Kennedy, who in the
months before his death had begun to speak out
strongly on the moral issue of racial equality, has been
compared to Lincoln. To the Negro people of Albany
however, he often seemed a reluctant Emancipator.
Those 1,200 Albany Negroes and their white friends
who spent time in prison in 1961 and 1962 tried with
the sheer weight of their numbers to act as a substitute
for the federal government in enforcing the Constitution of the United States.

The First Amendment of the Constitution of the
United States says: "Congress shall make no law . . .
abridging the freedom of speech or of the press; or of
the right of the people peaceably to assemble and to
petition the Government for a redress of grievances."
Supreme Court decisions have made it clear beyond
question that these rights of free speech, petition, and
assembly, are also guaranteed against state or local action by the warning of the Fourteenth Amendment, that
no state shall "deprive any person of life, liberty, or
property without due process of law." Yet in Albany,
hundreds of Negroes were locked up in some of the
most miserable jails in the country for peaceably attempting to petition the government for a redress of
grievances. Is the national government powerless to
protect the right of petition?

Section 242 of the U. S. Criminal Code, which comes

from the Civil Rights Act of 1866 and the Enforcement
Act of 1870, creates a legal basis for federal prosecution of: "Whoever, under color of any law . . . wil-
fully subjects . . . any inhabitant of any State . . .
to the deprivation of any rights, privileges, or immuni-
ties secured or protected by the Constitution and laws
of the United States . . ." Three times in succession in
November and December 1961, the police of the city
of Albany, by arresting Negroes and whites in connection with their use of the terminal facilities in that city,
violated a right which has been made clear beyond a
shadow of doubt in the courts, and nailed down tight by
a ruling of the Interstate Commerce Commission. Yet,
the federal government took no action.

When a sheriff, in the presence of witnesses, slapped
a young Negro for claiming the right to sing and pray in
prison, the federal government was silent. Throughout
the December troubles, there were telephone calls from
the Department of Justice to Governor Vandiver and
Mayor Kelley, conversations between the Department
and leaders of the Albany Movement. The FBI dutifully sat in its office in Albany and took dozens upon
dozens of affidavits from Negro citizens complaining
that their constitutional rights had been violated by city
and county officials. But eight months later, there was
not a sign of action on these charges.

In the spring and summer of 1962, hundreds of Negroes, and some whites, were again deprived of their
constitutional rights by city and county officials. They
were put into jail again and again for taking actions
supposedly protected by the First and Fourteenth
Amendments. A pregnant woman was beaten, a lawyer
was caned, a white youth had his jaw and ribs broken,

three young people were forcibly dragged from a court-
room under the eyes of a county judge. Still no action.
Cordell Reagan said to me, in near desperation,
"They're letting them get away with murder."

In December 1961, in the midst of hundreds of jailings in the Albany demonstrations, *The New York
Times* reported from Albany: "The Justice Department
was watching developments here closely." Nine
months later, after shotgun blasts ripped into a home
in Terrell County where Negro and white registration
workers were staying, a Department of Justice spokesman said in Washington: "We are watching the situation
very, very closely."

In June 1962, six months after several flagrant violations of the ICC ruling, the *Atlanta Journal's* Washington correspondent reported: "The U. S. Justice Department has launched an investigation of alleged bus
station segregation in Albany." In July, several Department of Justice lawyers were sent to Albany. On the
26th of that month, according to an *Atlanta Constitution* report, Albany's Mayor Kelley conferred in Washington with Attorney General Robert Kennedy. The
Constitution said: "Kelley said he told Kennedy that Albany's racial problems are dealt with by local people.
Kelley said Kennedy agreed with him."

Douglas Kiker, the *Atlanta Journal's* Washington
correspondent, reported in July: "Justice Department
officials described the Albany trouble Monday as 'a
tense situation' but added that Mayor Asa Kelley and
Chief of Police Laurie Pritchett 'have certainly indicated a strong desire to maintain order.' They said they
had received no evidence that Albany police are not
furnishing adequate law protection." This was im-

mediately after Attorney C. B. King, with more than 100 city and county police nearby, had received his bloody beating at the hands of the Dougherty County Sheriff. Kiker disclosed that the Department of Justice was "investigating" the beating of King. But if there was ever a case where one hour of investigation would be sufficient to establish grounds for federal action, this was it.

Near the end of the summer, after receiving dozens of angry telegrams, after the picketing of the White House by citizens from both North and South, and after face-to-face pleas from Roy Wilkins of the NAACP and William Kunstler of the American Civil Liberties Union, the Department of Justice made two legal moves: first, it entered a friend-of-the-court brief to support the Albany Movement's request that an injunction against further demonstrations be denied; and second, it asked for an injunction (after a violation of voting rights in Terrell County so outrageous that usually calm reporters on the scene were upset) to prevent certain officials in Southeast Georgia from interfering with voter-registration activities.

President Kennedy's first substantive public statement came after eight months of trouble in Albany. Responding to a question at his August 1, 1961, press conference, he called the situation "unsatisfactory," declared he could not understand why Albany city officials would not negotiate with Negroes, and said: "We are going to attempt as we have in the past to try to provide a satisfactory solution for the protection of the constitutional rights of the people of Albany, and we will continue to do so."

In another press conference on Thursday, September

4, 1962, again in response to a question, President Kennedy strongly denounced the burning of the Negro churches in Lee and Terrell Counties, calling the actions "cowardly as well as outrageous." This was commendable. But it also indicates the level of tolerance at which our national leaders—like most white Americans —operate. They are aroused by open violence, particularly against places of worship. But they are not made sufficiently indignant by mass jailings, by the deprivation of free speech and assembly, by beatings and intimidation, by the perpetuation of segregation. The nation as a whole has needed to expand its capacity for outrage.

Only once in the Albany troubles did the national administration show a real burst of energy; that was when Martin Luther King, Jr., was jailed on July 10. The President asked for a report, the Attorney General got busy, the Assistant Attorney General in charge of civil rights made telephone calls, and the next day King was out of jail. But there was no such deep concern for the hundreds of ordinary citizens in Albany who went to jail about the same time for basically the same reason.

The President's general silence and the feebleness with which the Department of Justice acted were sometimes attributed to the practical realities of national politics, which require, it is said, that the President woo the support of Southerners in Congress for other laudable national goals. But there are some means so morally hurtful that they corrupt the ends. Besides, there is serious reason to doubt that the administration gained substantial advantage from such tactics. The Senators from the state of Georgia, throughout 1961 and 1962, consistently voted against the administration on important issues.

The available administrative machinery for enforcing federal law should be outlined: The Department of Justice has the duty to enforce the laws passed by Congress and the provisions of the United States Constitution. In the Department there is a Civil Rights Division, headed by an Assistant Attorney General, which handles the bulk of the legal work of the Department dealing with civil rights cases. The Division depends for its information on another branch of the Department of Justice, the Federal Bureau of Investigation, which has offices in cities all over the country. FBI agents undertake investigations on orders from the Department to determine if federal law has been violated. The FBI can make arrests, usually on orders from the Department, sometimes on its own in urgent situations. After investigation, in civil rights cases, it is up to the Civil Rights Division to decide whether prosecution should be initiated. If so, this is usually done through the United States Attorney in that judicial district, who prosecutes the case in Federal District Court, after indictment by a grand jury or the filing of an information. Also upon the Department's advice or order, United States Attorney may file civil suits (although this may be done by a Civil Rights Division lawyer from Washington) that ask the federal court to issue injunctions which forbid certain parties to engage in specified practices which may deprive individuals of their rights under the Constitution. Attached to the Federal District Court are United States Marshals, who serve subpoenas, give notice of injunctive action, and otherwise carry out the orders of the court or the Attorney General. From District Court, there is the right of appeal to the Court of Appeals, and then, in certain cases, to the United States Supreme Court.

Clearly, in such a scheme, the Federal Bureau of Investigation is important. But there is considerable distrust among Albany Negroes for local members of the FBI. "They're a bunch of racists," a young Negro told me bitterly. Even if distorted, the statement is a general reflection of the efficacy of the FBI's role in the area of civil rights. FBI men appear to Albany Negroes as vaguely interested observers of injustice, who diffidently write down complaints and do no more. With all the clear violations by local police of constitutional rights, with undisputed evidence of beatings by sheriffs and deputy sheriffs, the FBI did not make a single arrest on behalf of Negro citizens.

In its 1961 volume, *Justice,* the Commission on Civil Rights implied that the FBI may be fundamentally incapable of enforcing the civil rights of American citizens. This is so because of its natural attachment to local police, on whom it is dependent for the solution of ordinary crimes, and because it is these same local police who are the most frequent violators of the rights of Negroes in the South.

Through 1963 and into early 1964, the police in Albany continued to violate the First and Fourteenth Amendments with no interference from the national government. In the summer of 1963, six people passing out leaflets dealing with a bond issue vote "were hustled off to jail as summarily as if they had been putting dynamite under City Hall" reported Reese Cleghorn, an Atlanta newspaperman, in the *New Republic.* In the fall a group of peace walkers, who were also distributing handbills on the street, were thrown into prison. "It's a police state we live in here," says Slater King about his home town.

It is the executive branch of our government—the President, the Attorney General, the Department of Justice, the FBI—which has the moral and legal responsibility of enforcing the Constitution and laws of the nation. Since Northern and Southern politicians ended Radical Reconstruction by a political deal in 1877, that responsibility has not been fulfilled in the Deep South. Now the Second Reconstruction, led by Negroes and therefore not so susceptible to withdrawal, confronts the executive branch with its duty once again.

There is no longer any excuse for putting it off on the courts or on Congress. The Supreme Court has spoken beyond the point of patience. Congress made the law plain in 1866 when it passed the Fourteenth Amendment, and reinforced it with several civil rights acts of that year, which make it a crime for a local official to deprive a person of his constitutional rights, or for anyone to conspire to that end (Section 241 and 242, Title 18, of the U. S. Code). So far, the executive branch has evaded its duty, not only in Albany, but in situation after situation all over the Black Belt, where jailings, beatings, and deprivation of First Amendment liberties face any challenger of the old order.

When accused of inaction, the Department of Justice points to the handful of suits it has taken into court, mostly in connection with voter-registration activities. These suits have been too few, too unimaginative, and too late. They are usually settled long after the fact. The crucial problems are *on-the-spot enforcement* of constitutional rights and *preventive* action. Two steps are urgent.

The first is to spread a network of injunctions all over the Deep South—secured in the courts by a bold and energetic group of Department of Justice attorneys—to warn all police officers, in advance, not to interfere with voting, with picketing, with leaflet distribution, with assembly, or any other form of peaceful activity protected by the Constitution. These injunctions would be powerful deterrents—because offenders would be immediately punishable by the court on grounds of contempt, without the lengthy procedure of criminal prosecution.

The Department of Justice has thus far insisted that it cannot ask for injunctions except in cases connected with voting, because it needs specific statutory authorization—provided in the case of voting by the Civil Rights Acts of 1957 and 1960. In other words, the Department says, it cannot go into federal court and ask for an order to prevent a police officer from interfering with the distribution of leaflets—a right protected under the First Amendment guarantee of freedom of the press—because it needs a specific congressional enactment that says it can do so.

The argument is a weak one, and it has been pulled apart by a number of experts in constitutional law (see, for instance, Jack Greenberg's *Race Relations and American Law*). The judicial rock which the Department of Justice keeps ignoring and which, if used as an anchor, could lead to a barrage of injunctions, is the *Debs Case* of 1895. In that case there was no specific legislative basis for an injunction; yet the Supreme Court ruled that the federal government could get one: "Every government . . . has a right to apply to its own courts" in matters which the Constitution has put within the jurisdiction of the national government. The Court said:

> The entire strength of the nation may be used to enforce in any part of the land the full and free exercise of all national powers and the security of all rights entrusted by the Constitution to its care.

The government may choose to interpret its own powers narrowly, or it may interpret them broadly. The degree of its compassion may dictate the choice. When the present reluctance of the Department of Justice to act is combined with the unhesitant exercise of power by local police, the result is a blinding of the First and Fourteenth Amendments with the first flash of a police officer's badge.

Civil rights legislation passed in 1964 may give the Department of Justice the statutory authorization it wants, but even that will not make a decisive change unless the President and the Attorney General *want* to challenge the police dictatorships of the Black Belt.

The second necessary step is to establish a federal presence in the Black Belt to protect citizens from intimidation, beating, and false arrest. This would mean stationing a substantial force of federal agents in various parts of the Deep South. These agents would not confine themselves to standing by and taking notes, as the FBI has been doing in the midst of scenes of brutality; they would have the authority to make arrests on the spot. Like the T-men of the Treasury Department (these might be called E-men, for Equality), they would have a specific function, to protect civil rights.

The FBI is most effective as an agency for the solution of ordinary crimes, and perhaps it should stick to that.

Burke Marshall, Assistant Attorney General in charge of the Civil Rights Division of the Department of Justice, has been opposed to discussing "a national police force or some other extreme alternative." But the FBI is exactly that, a national police force, designed to investigate and apprehend criminals who violate federal laws. Does not a violation of the civil rights statutes, or of the Fourteenth Amendment or the First Amendment, call as urgently for federal action as a bank robbery or driving a stolen car across a state line? Why are FBI agents, who are authorized to make arrests when they see a federal crime being committed, held back by higher-ups in the executive branch from making such arrests in civil rights violations? True, J. Edgar Hoover is not known as a vigorous spokesman for racial equality, but the problem seems to go beyond him—to the cabinet, to the presidency, to political gamesmanship and moral failure.

Another argument used by Burke Marshall and others against the E-men is that such forceful action by the national government would be a break from our "federal system." This is a pre-Civil War view of federalism, for it was precisely the purpose of the Fourteenth Amendment to take the enforcement of racial equality out of the hands of local governments, which had proved the most flagrant violators, and to put the ultimate authority in the hands of the nation.

Federalism is a division of power, and the Constitution sets the rules for the division. Once the Fourteenth Amendment was passed, the prohibition of racial discrimination moved over to the national side of the fed-

eral arrangement. Local governments may do anything they want in the field of ordinary crime. They
may punish people for disorderly conduct, for blocking
sidewalks, for disobeying police officers. But the moment such police action is obviously being used as a
weapon for maintaining segregation, the Fourteenth
Amendment is violated and the federal government,
with all the power at its command, has proper constitutional jurisdiction.

Some opponents of a new federal presence in the
South accept both the necessity and the legality of such
a force, but argue that it will lead to armed conflict.
This, I submit, is to ignore that hierarchy of values in
the Southern mind, in which segregation may rank
quite high, but the desire to stay out of trouble with the
law ranks higher. Those very few white Southerners
who value segregation above their freedom may end
up in jail; most will obey the law, once firmly enforced.
Even Governor Wallace of Alabama and Governor
Barnett of Mississippi, who swore defiance to the end
against federal authority, gave way before court orders
backed by armed force. Once the pattern of Southern
life begins to change, white Southerners will adapt, in
that extraordinary way people everywhere adapt to
changed circumstances. And because the change will
be more in keeping with the national ideal, and with the
common interest of *all* Southerners, it will stick.

Another assumption of the executive branch has
been that there is no need for vigorous federal action
so long as large-scale violence does not break out—no
matter how many Negroes are sent to jail for peaceful
protest—and so long as local police maintain "order."
But if the government's only requirement is the main-
tenance of "order," even without the existence of free-

dom, then we have moved close to the ideology of the totalitarian state.

To reinforce the two suggestions made above—injunctions based on the *Debs Case* and the creation of the E-men—it would be good to have the President stop the practice of appointing segregationist federal judges in the Deep South. True, this would require a radical departure from the tradition which calls for the President, when making an appointment in Georgia for instance, to consult Senators Russell and Talmadge, with the result that judges like Elliott are appointed in Albany. But the Kennedy-Johnson administration did promise a "New Frontier." As yet, no new frontiers have been carved out in the social wilderness that surrounds Albany.

In the summer of 1963, the passive role played by the federal government in the Albany racial crisis abruptly turned into one of dynamic action: the Department of Justice initiated its first large-scale criminal prosecution—against eight Negro leaders and a white student in the Albany Movement. It was a strange turn of events, after almost three years in which the Department of Justice stood by while Chief Pritchett put Albany Negroes and their constitutional rights in jail.

It all arose out of an incident that took place in "Bad Baker" County in 1961. A handcuffed Negro named Charlie Ware was shot four times while being taken into custody by Sheriff Warren L. Johnson. Ware, charging a violation of his civil rights under federal law, sued the Sheriff for $125,000. At the trial, held in Macon in April 1963, an all-white jury dismissed the claim.

One of the jurors was Carl Smith, who owned a

supermarket in Albany. Businessmen in Albany had been picketed for over a year as part of a general boycott by the Albany Movement, but when Carl Smith's store was picketed, shortly after the Ware trial ended, FBI agents seemed to be swarming all over the place. The picket signs asked that Smith hire Negroes in his store; no signs mentioned the Ware trial. Curiously enough, after one day of picketing, Carl Smith—who had been grossing over $200,000 a year—closed up the store and moved out, "driven out of business" by the picketing, thus establishing a perfect federal case. It was apparently the most effective bit of picketing in the history of the civil rights struggle.

A federal grand jury, meeting in Macon in early August, called before it various members of the Albany Movement, including one white college student, Joni Rabinowitz, who was carrying out her Antioch College work-study assignment by doing voter-registration work in the Albany area. Eighteen of the twenty-three grand jurors were white, but the votes of only twelve persons were needed to indict.

On August 9, 1963, the grand jury handed down nine indictments. Dr. William C. Anderson, former president of the Albany Movement, and two other members of the Movement, were indicted on charges of conspiring to obstruct justice by picketing and boycotting Smith's supermarket—a federal offense calling for up to ten years imprisonment. Five Negroes, including Slater King (who had replaced Anderson as president of the Albany Movement) and Mrs. Eliza Jackson (the Movement's secretary-treasurer), were indicted for perjury, for denying they were at a meeting in their lawyer's office to discuss the grand jury hearings. Joni Rab-

inowitz was indicted on three counts of perjury for saying that she was not at the picketing of Smith's store,
she did not see the picketing, she did not know about
the picketing.

At pre-trial hearings, attorneys for the defendants
pointed out that their clients were not likely to get fair
trials from all-white juries in Georgia. The Department
of Justice—which in previous instances had explained
its reluctance to prosecute Southern policemen who had
beaten Negroes, on the ground that all-white juries
would not judge the issue fairly—now denied that these
trials would be unfair. All of the defendants who were
tried were found guilty, with the exception of Dr. Anderson, in whose case three jurors held out and created
a hung trial; the government immediately moved for a
retrial. Slater King was sentenced to a year and a day in
prison, as was Rev. Samuel Wells, one of the great
church-meeting orators of the Albany Movement. Joni
Rabinowitz was sentenced to three months to four
years.

During the trials, United States Attorney Floyd Buford said that "at least thirty-eight" FBI agents had
worked on the prosecutions. Never, during all the beatings and jailings of the past two years, had there been
that many FBI agents in evidence in Albany.

Clearly, these prosecutions could not have been undertaken without the approval of Attorney General
Robert Kennedy. A representative of the Department
of Justice came down from Washington to sit with the
United States Attorney during the trials. Those Negroes
drawn for possible jury service were removed by the
peremptory challenge of the government of the United
States.

Civil rights lawyers tended to agree with the judgment of Attorney William L. Kunstler, who called the trials "a bone thrown to the segregationists" by the administration. Attorney Shad Polier, of the American Jewish Congress, in a biting analysis of the government's action, called it all "a misuse of the power of the Federal Government to pander to local prejudice."

It was an irony of shattering proportions. My own reaction was to think immediately of Slater King, whom I had interviewed in Albany right after the beating of his wife by deputy sheriffs, and who had spoken of the indifference of the FBI men who were investigating her complaint. He had been jailed and physically abused and his brother had received a bloody caning at the hands of the sheriff—none of this punished by federal action. Then his wife had lost the baby she was carrying at the time she was beaten. Now the government was trying to put him in jail for a year. I thought also of the title of a World War I case involving government censorship of a motion picture: *The United States v. "The Spirit of '76."*

The Albany indictments represent the most striking evidence thus far that the rights of Negroes do not stand near the top of the national government's set of priorities. It is probably true that the government itself—throughout the nation's history—has been a victim of the mystique surrounding the South; it does not understand the determination of the New Negro and does not fathom the potential receptivity of the white man. But it is also true that many of the nation's citizens have fallen prey to a mystique about the nation's leaders, one which sees as their top priority—particularly when the heads of government are "liberals"—moral concern.

In the next part, I shall discuss where our nation as a whole has stood historically on the issue of race—and on other moral issues. For now, I simply want to note that, because of the self-imposed limitations of the national government, there is a vast no-man's land for American Negroes, into which they are invited by the Constitution, but where federal authority will not protect them. The mystique is toxic. The only antidote, not used thus far by the government, is the existentialist demand: *act*.

If there is a quality of harshness in my estimate of a federal government so often lauded by liberals, it may come from some of the things I heard and saw in the Albany area. I recall particularly driving from dirt road onto dirt road deep into the cotton and peanut land of Lee County to talk to James Mays, a teacher and farmer. He showed me the damage done by 30 bullets which hours before, in the middle of the night, had been fired through doors and windows and had crashed into the walls around the heads of 19 sleeping persons, most of them children. With the coming of dawn, he had quickly lettered a sign of protest and stood with it out on the main road to Leesburg in front of a Negro school. It was clear that, although he was a member of a nation whose power stretched around the globe and into space, James Mays was on his own.

PART FOUR

The South as a Mirror

Deep-set in the Southern mystique is the notion that the South is more than just "different," that it is distinct from the rest of the nation—a sport, a freak, an inexplicable variant from the national norm. The South, so it goes, does more than *speak* differently; it *thinks* differently. Its apartness goes deeper than the visible elements of soil and sun and large black populations, into the innermost values of the region, into what Wilbur J. Cash called "The Mind of the South." The South—and we are drawn to agree by each ugly headline—has its own set of characteristics. Racism tops the list, of course. But the South is also provincial, conservative, fundamentalist, nativist, violent, conformist, militarist. It is a stranger to the nation, and not even four years of bloodletting could wash away that strangeness.

Such is the American mystique about the South; and it feeds self-righteousness in the North, defiance below the Mason-Dixon Line. It is supported (deliberately, or unwittingly) by legions of writers, by William Faulkner, by Erskine Caldwell, by Tennessee Williams. And it stands so firmly and so high on a ledge of truth that one must strain to see the glitter of deception in its eye.

For the South, I am about to argue, far from being utterly different, is really the *essence* of the nation. It is not a mutation born by some accident into the normal, lovely American family; it has simply taken the national genes and done the most with them. It contains, in concentrated and dangerous form, a set of characteristics which mark the country as a whole. It is different because it is a distillation of those traits which are the worst (and a few which are the best) in the national character. Those very qualities long attributed to the South as special possessions are, in truth, *American* qualities, and the nation reacts emotionally to the South precisely because it subconsciously recognizes itself there. The mystery is that attached to the bastard child, whose father disavows his act. But a paternity test, I suspect, would destroy the charge of bastardy and reveal the United States as the true father of the Southern region.

Because the South embarrasses us, we try to disown it, apologize for it, hold it at a distance, pretend it is an abnormal growth on the national body. Once, however, we face the truth—that the South crystallizes the defects of the nation—there may be some value in the acknowledgment. In this part, I shall examine a number of these traits alleged to be peculiarly Southern. Then I shall suggest how candid self-recognition by the nation can be an occasion not for shame, but for insight, and how the South, miserable and rejected, may yet turn out to be the savior of the American dream.

We start, of course, with racism. The ugliest bastions of racist thought and action are in the South: that is undisputed. But when the white Southerner tries to lighten

the burden of his guilt by pointing to prejudice and discrimination in the North, the equalitarians, while con-
tinuing to denounce the South, become uneasy, for
they know how much truth is in the accusation. Although the symptoms show mostly in the South, the entire mind and body of the American nation are afflicted.
And it may be important, exactly at this moment in our
history, when the South is going through the early
stages of a kind of shock therapy, for the rest of the nation to understand that it stands by not as an adminis-
tering doctor, but as the next patient in line. The South
turned out to be a convenient place—a kind of Fort
Knox of prejudice—where the nation has always stored
the bulk of its bigotry, while the rest has circulated—
though sometimes stealthily—all over the country.

Slavery, because of favorable agricultural conditions,
was concentrated in the American South, but it existed everywhere in the American colonies for over a
hundred years. Slaves worked on the land in Rhode Island and New York by the thousands. In the mid-
seventeenth century, around the same time that slavery had become a legal institution in Virginia and Maryland, it was legitimized in New York, and it was a
fact of life in every Northern colony. On the eve of the
Revolution, New York had over 15,000 slaves, roughly
10 per cent of the population. New York law in the
eighteenth century provided that any slave caught trav-
eling forty miles above Albany would be executed upon
the oath of two credible witnesses. In 1712, a slave up-
rising took place in New York, when a group of armed
Negro slaves killed nine white men. Awaiting capture
by the militia, four cut their own throats and one shot
his wife and then himself. Twenty-one were executed.

A woman was hanged; one man was broken on the wheel and quartered; some were burned to death.

New York again became the scene of race terror in 1741 when a series of fires led to wild rumors of insurrection and to a hysterical trial, which convicted a hundred Negroes and four whites of conspiracy to take over the city. The four whites, one of whom was accused of wanting to establish a monarchy in New York with himself as king and a Negro named Caesar as governor, were hanged. Eighteen Negroes were hanged. Thirteen other Negroes were burned alive. One account reads: "At the rate of two every week, one hanged, and one burned alive, the victims were executed amid prayers, imprecations, and shrieks of agony."

New Jersey, twenty-four years after the Declaration of Independence, had 1,000 slaves; in 1741 the state burned two Negroes at the stake for setting fire to seven barns in Hackensack. Pennsylvania, the Quaker State, famed for its tolerance of Negroes, had 3,700 slaves in 1790. Negroes were tried by special courts in that state, and were not allowed to assemble in groups of more than four.

In New England, the source of so much abolitionist agitation, slavery was well-established in the first generation of colonization. Those celebrating the heritage of Puritan New England speak fondly of the "Body of Liberties" adopted in Massachusetts in 1641. This prohibited slavery "unless it be lawful captives taken in just wars, and such strangers as willingly sell themselves or are sold to us." In other words, the enslavement of people was obnoxious—except through war or commerce. It is as clear an example of Puritan hypocrisy as we have, and a striking example of the emptiness of Northern moralizing.

When Southerners, stung by Northern posturing, retorted that their slaves had been brought to them by Yankee traders, they were telling the truth. It was an accident of geography and economics, rather than a different attitude of mind or a different capacity to tolerate evil, that kept the number of slaves relatively low in the North. It was the immediate situation—particularly the spur of profit—rather than any persistent difference in regional history or psychology, that determined the extent of enslavement.

The state-by-state abolition of slavery in the North after the Revolution did not signify the abolition of racism; it merely ended one special form of it. For the key factor which ended slavery in the North was not a significant breaking down of racial attitudes, but a set of circumstances which made slavery unprofitable and inconvenient. That these circumstances were heightened by some of the ideological ferment of the Declaration of Independence and the Revolution I would not deny, but ideology played, I believe, only a marginal role. Certainly, moral considerations may tip the scales of social decision, but their weight is usually so slight that they can do this only when the scales are already closely balanced by harder considerations of self-interest. Specifically, it was in the interest of winning the war that the Continental Army enlisted 5,000 Negroes, promising freedom to many after victory over England.

Differences existed between the sections. Abolitionists could not operate at all in the South after the 1830's. In the North they could speak and print—but at the risk of their lives. Garrison was mobbed in Boston, Phillips was stoned throughout the North, and Lovejoy was murdered in Illinois. Stephen Foster was twice

thrown from a second story window by angry Northerners for preaching abolition. "These dangerous men
must be met. They agitate a question that must not be
tampered with," said a Boston newspaper.

It was in Connecticut that schoolmistress Prudence
Crandall was jailed for admitting a Negro girl to her
Academy. The school's well was filled with manure,
the local druggist refused to sell her medicine, fires
broke out in the building, and finally men with iron
bars and heavy clubs wrecked the school.

Negroes were enslaved in the South and they were
segregated in the North. Ohio barred Negroes from its
public schools until 1849, then gave them separate,
impoverished schools. Violence against Negroes (a Negro woman stoned to death in Philadelphia, riots in
Portsmouth, Ohio, and in Cincinnati, racial outbursts in
Utica, New York, and in New York City, mob violence
elsewhere) was only the most visible tip of a punishing
rod that was used against Negroes in the North in every
aspect of their day-to-day lives.

Fanny Kemble, who knew the Southern situation
well, reported on the Northern Negroes as follows:
"They are not slaves indeed, but they are pariahs, de-
barred from every fellowship save with their own de-
spised race. . . . All hands are extended to thrust
them out, all fingers point at their dusky skin, all
tongues . . . have learned to turn the very name of
their race into an insult and a reproach."

John Hope Franklin's chapter on the "free" Negro,
in *From Slavery to Freedom,* is entitled "Quasi-Free
Negroes"; this is closer to the truth. When "free" Negroes met in Rochester in 1853 under the leadership of
Frederick Douglass, they issued a memorial saying

that "with the exception of the Jews, under the whole heavens, there is not to be found a people pursued with a more relentless prejudice and persecution, than are the free colored people of the United States."

My object here is not to deny the difference in quantity, or even in the intensity, of mistreatment, but to point to what is too often overlooked: the basic community of interest of all sections of the United States, reaching back to our earliest history and extending through our entire national experience, in racist outlook and practice. The "American dilemma" of which Gunnar Myrdal and others spoke has never been the tension between an American dream and Southern reality, but between the American dream and national reality.

We are all somewhat befogged by the spell which history has cast over the Civil War and Abraham Lincoln. The abolition of slavery, although a prime motive among the thousands of Abolitionists, was more often secondary or non-existent as a motive for those millions of white people in the North who backed Lincoln. The drums of war and the hymns to John Brown barely covered the sound of rioting in the streets of New York in 1863 against the draft, and the lynching of Negroes in those riots.

In his debates with Stephen Douglas, Lincoln had expressed his belief that the Negro should be assigned an inferior place in society. And although he was against the extension of slavery, Lincoln did not favor interfering with slavery in the Southern states. True, this crass summing up does not do justice to the strain of humanism in Lincoln's thought, but it is a large part of the truth about Lincoln. The Emancipation Proclama-

tion, Richard Hofstadter has reminded us, "had all the
moral grandeur of a bill of lading." And when former
slave Frederick Douglass dedicated the Freedman's
Monument in 1876, he spoke candidly and pointed
out that white men were the true children of Lincoln.
Negroes, he told the crowd, "are at best only his step-
children, children by adoption, children by force of circumstance and necessity."

At the end of the Civil War, only five of the twenty-
four Northern states allowed Negroes to vote. Even the
first excitement of victory could not induce the others
to act: in 1865 and 1866, eight Northern states turned
down proposals to let Negroes vote.

We associate the Reconstruction period with Northern insistence on equal rights and Southern brutality toward the Negro. It was not moral fervor, however, as
much as the political interest of the Republican party,
that established Radical Reconstruction in the South for
a half dozen years or so. The equalitarianism of Thad-
deus Stevens and Charles Sumner was a minority view-
point in the North during this time. There was another
view, represented by people like Congressman Mor-
rissey of New York, who argued, a few years after
Appomattox, against appropriating money for the
Freedman's Bureau:

> Mr. Speaker, the glorious charter of our liber-
> ties, the Constitution of the United States, says
> that all men are created equal, and now sir, I
> should like to know where in the document you
> can find one word about the nigger; damn the nig-
> ger . . . Is the nigger mentioned at all? and
> wouldn't our forefathers have said something

about him if they thought he was worth mention-
ing at all? Damn the nigger! Mr. Speaker, was
George Washington a nigger? Was General Put-
nam, or any hero of the Revolution, except Bene-
dict Arnold, who ought to have been one?

In the same period in Michigan, during the drafting
of a new state constitution, there was much debate over
the question of Negro suffrage. The Detroit *Free Press*
warned that if Negroes were given the vote, "the mass
approaching polls in each election day will resemble in
complexion the dancing witches in Macbeth" and announced on its pages that summer of 1867: "Negroes
and Savages to be allowed to vote."

I cite these quotations, not to assert exactly what
were the mass sentiments of the population, for these
cannot be demonstrated by quotation, but to make it
clear that racism was prominent in the North too during
the Reconstruction period. It was possible to sustain the
Radical Reconstruction governments in the South, even
for that short period, only because a small but solid
core of white Southerners recognized Negro equality,
at least in politics. That the motivation here was to a
large extent selfish places them exactly in the same
position as most of the self-righteous Reconstruction-
ists of the North. There is no sectional boundary, apparently, either to moral rectitude or to political ambition.

If racism depends, as I have said, on the visibility of
physical difference accompanied by some grievance,
then it is always at the edge of possibility in the North
as well as in the South. The ghetto of Harlem has been
as real, as terrible, as any colored section of a Deep

South city. In New York City in the 1930's, the pattern
of Negro life was hardly distinguishable from Atlanta
in the 1960's. Negroes lived on their own streets, often in the darkness under the "el." They emerged
from rat-infested tenements in the early morning to
work as maids and janitors in the white neighborhoods,
then came back at dusk to supper, children, and the
second-hand radio. And is it much changed today?
James Baldwin, out of his Harlem years, says: "For
the Negro there's no difference between North and
South. There's only a difference in *the way* they castrate
you."

I have heard countless arguments among Negroes
about which is a better place to live, North or South.
The steady stream of migration northward provides
proof that there *is* a difference, and the anxiety of
young Southern Negroes to leave home after their
schooling is further corroboration. True: "Up North
they do it behind your back. Down here it's to your
face." But there are avenues of protest and sources of
power for the Negro in the North that are non-existent
in much of the South.

It is a complex truth, and there are certain times
when it is useful to focus on the difference between the
sections, other times when there is social value in noting the similarity. It is in the interest of a longer perspective that I come back to my point: there is no part
of the United States where Negroes as a group have ever
stood as equals with whites.

National politics has always reflected, as it does today, the racist thread in American thought. The excuse
that this is due to Southern influence in national government is a fragile one, because such influence has
rarely met powerful resistance.

In those times that vigorous moves were made by the national government against the South they were not primarily on behalf of the Negro, but because other needs pulled irresistibly: the unity of the nation, in the Civil War; the political supremacy of Republicanism, in the Reconstruction period; the economic recovery of the nation, during the early years of the New Deal; our world position, in the 1960's.

Do we have in our national history any evidence of the federal government, *on its own initiative,* moving forcefully to fulfill the words of the Declaration of Independence, or, later, of the Fourteenth Amendment? Always it has been tons of sweat and protest poured into a huge funnel by angry Negroes and sympathetic whites and emerging from the narrow spout of national politics in trickles of action. This was true of Lincoln during abolitionist days, and of Kennedy during freedom-ride and sit-in days.

The removal of Jefferson's anti-slavery paragraph from the Declaration of Independence marks the very beginning of that blight of compromise and timidity which has been a national characteristic when dealing with the question of race. It is one of the ironies of our war for "freedom" against England that we closed it with demands for the return of slaves taken from the South by the British. The Negro has always been third or sixteenth or last in the national list of priorities— never first.

It is a sign of our national preoccupation with interests other than the Negro that Andrew Jackson is considered one of the heroes of a rising American democracy. That Jackson fought against the Bank seems much more important to us than the fact that he was a slaveholder, and that he set himself firmly against abolitionist attempts to work for freedom. It was his administration, we might recall, which put a ban on sending abolitionist literature through the mails into the South.

The extension of Jackson's racism to the Indians was typically American. The assumption of white superiority over the Indians became embedded in our heritage despite the pleas of humanitarians like Roger Williams. Racism, as we have seen, sticks like glue to any situation which combines physical difference and some other strong interest. The position of the Indians, who were not only visibly different but culturally odd, and in possession of land resources that Americans coveted, invited a murderous series of attacks.

The Negro has always been a hitchhiker in American history. Left in the mud before the Civil War, the Negro was allowed to climb aboard with Lincoln for a while (sitting in the back) only because his destination coincided temporarily with that of the white drivers of the national vehicle. When their goals diverged (in the compromise of 1877), he was kicked off again, and it took the wars of the twentieth century to make the nation, in self-defense, give the Negro a lift once more. The kindnesses have come more often from Northern drivers than Southern ones. But this does not alter the essence of the Negro's status as a subordinate being whose progress, up to now, has depended on the pleasure of others. The revolution in the South today is precisely an attempt to change this status, and it is not so much an assault on the South as it is on the nation.

It is standard operating procedure for American presidents to blame the persistence of national discrimination on the South, and particularly on Southern power in Congress. Until the ratification of the Fourteenth

Amendment in 1868, our constitutional structure did
not permit national interference with racial discrimination. But since that time, the Constitution has in-
cluded the clause: "No State shall . . . deny to any
person within its jurisdiction the equal protection of
the laws." And since the decision of the Supreme Court
in the *Debs Case* of 1895, there has been a judicial
opening for the national government to use all the
power at its command to enforce any provision of the
Constitution. The picture, however, since that time is not
that of a vigorously equalitarian national government
balked by a determined South. It is rather that of a timo-
rous, compromising national leadership, unwilling to
press forward with the kind of power that could over-
ride the admittedly stubborn but far from omnipotent Southern resistance.

John F. Kennedy's campaign speeches in 1960 demanded strong leadership in the Presidency. The office,
he said, would "demand more than ringing mani-
festos from the rear of the battle. It will demand the
President place himself in the thick of the fight . . ."
But he had hardly been elected when he began to yield
on civil rights.

In December of 1960, the incoming Senate took a crucial vote. Liberals proposed to change the Senate rules
to make a filibuster more difficult by eliminating the requirement of a two-thirds vote for closing debate. The
motion to change the rules lost by four votes. Washington newspaperwoman Doris Fleeson, despite her obvious sympathy for Kennedy, called it "remarkable
. . . that he did not make the slightest effort to help
Democratic senators committed to his program win
their fight to end the filibuster. . . . With only a very

modest effort, the incoming President could have persuaded two Democrats to switch their vote against the
filibuster curb. This would have meant a tie, which
would have been resolved by Vice President Richard
Nixon in favor of the change. Change is now almost
surely postponed another four years at least. . . ."

In his book *Kennedy in Power*, James T. Crown says
that Kennedy made an agreement, before he took office, to push for no civil rights legislation in the first session of Congress, in return for legislative support on
other parts of his program. Florida's Senator Smathers,
a friend of Kennedy's, said plainly that Kennedy showed
no concern about changing the Senate rules in that crucial opening session.

When the Democratic caucus met in January 1961 to
map out strategy, with Kennedy now in the White
House, Senator Joseph Clark of Pennsylvania, a vigorous spokesman for civil rights, tried to find a prec-
edent for changing the committee structure so that it
would not be dominated by Southerners. When a member of his staff was denied access to the minutes of past
caucuses by Bobby Baker, the secretary to the Democratic caucus, Clark dug personally into those old records. He discovered that in the opening session of
1913, after a long conference with Woodrow Wilson, reform Democrats had eliminated twenty-eight ranking
Democrats from committee chairmanships and substi-
tuted men who would favor Wilson's program. The result was a series of sweeping reform measures passed
by Congress in 1913–14, a legislative corroboration of
Wilson's New Freedom.

The Wilsonian thrust at congressional tradition was
on behalf of certain economic issues. No such boldness

has been shown, either by Wilson or by any other administration, in the field of civil rights for Negroes.

Whatever reputations United States presidents have
had for courage were not in connection with the race
question but with other issues. Andrew Jackson fought
the politicians of South Carolina on the tariff, and the
moguls of the United States Bank on economics. Lincoln's daring was based on the desire for national political unity; he was most cautious on the race question. Theodore Roosevelt's bluster was in the field
of foreign affairs; he could wave the big stick at every
country in the Caribbean, but not at those Southerners
who protested his inviting Booker T. Washington to the
White House. Wilson's fortitude was on economic legislation and on the League of Nations. Franklin Roosevelt's reputation as a fighter came from his economic
policy in his early administrations and from foreign affairs later on.

Compromise and vacillation on the race question are
intrinsic parts of our national political heritage. Vocif-
erous as it may be, the South is still much less than a majority of the country and is economically backward
enough to be susceptible to pressure. The failure of national political action against racism, therefore, is attributable to national weakness rather than to Dixie
strength. The power of the South is sufficient to deter a
hesitant executive, but not a determined one. We will
only be able to prove this, it seems, when we get one.

The shocking assassination of John F. Kennedy, in
the midst of what seemed to be a tortured reappraisal
inside the White House of civil rights policy, makes one
hesitant to write critically of his Presidency. Yet it does
no service to that ultimate moral concern which Ken-

nedy often revealed, to refrain from appraising his administration honestly.

Compromise is self-perpetuating, because means tend to swallow ends. Kennedy played it cautious to win the nomination, then to win the election, then to get desired legislation in the 87th Congress, then to get desired legislation in the 88th Congress, and by this time he was so close to the 1964 presidential campaign that it was time to begin a second round of compromises, which was then interrupted by the sensational Negro mass protests of early 1963 and an abrupt reconsideration of political strategy.

One day Kennedy invited Martin Luther King, Jr., to the White House; another day he invited Alabama's racist Governor John Patterson. He appointed liberal Mennen Williams to deal with Africa, and made white-supremacist Charles Meriweather Director of the Export-Import Bank, which handles loans to some of the darker-skinned peoples of the world. The appointment of Thurgood Marshall to the Court of Appeals in New York was far less significant in the realities of civil rights combat (because *any* judge appointed in that circuit would be a strong defender of the Fourteenth Amendment) than his appointment of segregationist judges in Mississippi, Louisiana, and Georgia, where they have been significant obstacles to progress.

When criticized for inaction on civil rights, administration spokesmen blamed Congress, but the President was surprisingly shy in his relations with Congress. When Senator Clark proposed that no committee chairman be appointed whose views on issues before his committee were contrary to those platform planks adopted by the Party in 1960, he got no support from Kennedy. Instead of battling for a drastic reconstitution or enlargement of the all-powerful Rules Committee of the House, Kennedy settled for a modest enlargement from 12 to 15 members, so that not only civil rights legislation failed, but also his program on urban affairs, jobs for youth, and aid to colleges. One of the few pieces of civil rights legislation sponsored by the administration, a bill to prevent the application of literacy tests on racial lines, was filibustered to death in April 1962. Anthony Lewis wrote in *The New York Times:* "President Kennedy may have wanted the literacy bill as an abstract matter. But he said little on its behalf and did not act to make it a major public concern."

Although the national executive kept saying the ball was in the hands of Congress, whenever the ball did clearly fall into its own hands, it either got off a weak pass or fumbled completely. Vice President Lyndon Johnson had an opportunity, when the 88th Congress opened in January 1963, to support another move by a small group of liberal Senators for the amendment of Senate Rule 22 on cloture. Senator Anderson of New Mexico asked Johnson to rule that a filibuster could be ended by majority vote until rules were adopted for the new Congress. This would have prevented a filibuster on debate to change the rule. But Johnson refused to utilize his power as presiding officer to make this ruling, and the result was that the liberals, trying desperately to get a two-thirds vote to end the filibuster, fell short by ten votes. Then Johnson quickly recognized Mansfield's motion to adjourn, and the fight to change Rule 22 was over.

The name of Mansfield crops up again and again in the recent history of national weakness on civil rights. Mike Mansfield, Senator from Montana, was Kennedy's majority leader. From that first session in December 1960, Mansfield seemed reluctant to act to change Rule 22. When, on February 19, 1963, Senator Clark rose in the Senate to talk candidly about the "Senate Establishment," which he said dominated the fifteen-man Steering Committee of the Senate, Mansfield objected. It is Mansfield who appoints the members of that Steering Committee, and he took issue with Clark's statement that the South had an undue influence in this Committee. "I think," Mansfield said, "we ought to help our colleagues, no matter what part of the country they come from." The statement sounds reasonable on its face, but it often collides with another principle that should be more important to Mansfield: that the nation ought to help people, no matter what the color of their skins.

It was this Senate Steering Committee that decided on committee assignments. Nine of the fifteen men made chairmen of standing committees were Southerners. Senator Eastland was made chairman of the Judiciary Committee. The argument that seniority dictated this is countered by the evidence that seniority was ignored when Senators who had voted with the liberals against Rule 22 were kept from holding certain important committee posts. Punishment was used by the Steering Committee against liberals in a way that it was not used against racists.

The excuse for compromise with the Deep-South Senators was the necessity to win support for the administration's programs in areas other than civil rights.

But the record disposes quickly of this contention. Georgia is quite representative of the Deep South in this regard. Its two Senators, Richard Russell and Herman Talmadge, in votes on twelve key issues during 1961, both gave their support to Kennedy on exactly two of those twelve—and these were agricultural bills which Russell and Talmadge favored anyway. In 1962, out of eleven key issues, again only twice did both Russell and Talmadge take the side of the administration. One began to wonder how much of the hesitation of the national executive was due to "tactics," and how much to that historic national trait in the field of racial equality —diffidence.

When it became evident early in Kennedy's administration that he was not pushing Congress for action in the field of Negro rights, the justification was that he would depend on executive orders, which did not require Congressional consent. The most important issue here was the question of discrimination in housing. In his campaign Kennedy had railed against the Republicans for failing to wipe out discrimination in federally supported housing, which they could do, he said, "with a stroke of the pen." It turned out that Kennedy was an agonizingly slow writer himself. It took twenty-two months for him to affix his signature to the executive order on housing discrimination. And even after this came, in 1962, it was a compromise measure, short of the recommendations made by the Civil Rights Commission the previous year, and watered down even further when implementing regulations were added.

In early 1963, the administration could have used its executive power of the purse to discourage the children of servicemen from attending segregated schools. The

Department of Health, Education, and Welfare had been paying money to local school boards for such children who chose to attend segregated local schools rather than the integrated schools on the military bases. In February 1963, the Department decided to continue to underwrite with its funds such attendance at segregated schools, by paying about $150,000 to Houston County in Georgia and more money to other counties in the state.

It is true that under the Kennedys, the Civil Rights Division of the Department of Justice was expanded, and became more active than ever before. Still, it played a carefully limited role in the general upheaval shaking the South in 1961 and 1962. The Division made the decision, at some point, at someone's direction, to confine its judicial activity to the protection of the right to vote, with practically no activity in other matters affecting the Negro. In general, it did not take the initiative to desegregate facilities; it moved into a situation only in the face of imminent or actual violence to maintain "law and order," or it acted under the pressure of Negro protests.

In early 1963, following a storm of mass Negro demonstrations in Birmingham, Jackson, Albany, Savannah, Greensboro, Raleigh, and other Southern cities, the Kennedy administration took a sharp turn in its policy. The President, in a nationwide telecast, for the first time spoke eloquently and at length on the moral issues involved in the desegregation crisis. At the same time, his administration prepared to bring before Congress a bill to outlaw discrimination in public facilities throughout the nation; this became the Civil Rights Act of 1964.

That the pressure of world opinion, and the obvious power of Negro sentiment in this country, were the key factors in producing this change, should not detract from the praise due the national administration for its sensitivity in reacting as it did. But the argument is re-inforced, that the Negro is still not, in himself, a number one priority as a human problem. He must wait for considerations of politics and pressure to move the nation into giving him another lift on his way to full freedom. The Negro is learning, in the course of this Second Reconstruction of the past few years, that by taking to the streets, by demonstrating in the thousands, by bringing the issue to world attention, he can maneuver the national self-interest into alignment with his own needs. But there should be no delusion about the fact that political power rather than moral commitment is the primary motivating force of this national government, as of any national government, anywhere.

Another phenomenon of the spring and summer of 1963 was the spread of mass racial demonstrations for equality to the North: New York City, Englewood, Philadelphia, Chicago, and other cities. It was never made more plain that both racism and the battle against it are national rather than sectional in nature. One could not know from a picture in the newspaper showing a policeman hauling off a Negro to jail whether the scene was Birmingham or Brooklyn.

The President of the United States has an important choice open to him in any issue under dispute. He can either represent the nation's predominant views—or try to change them. Tremendous resources of opinion-molding are at his command, more today than ever before in history; in a single telecast he can speak to half the nation. On certain national problems, past presidents have chosen to lead the nation, as did Jackson, Wilson, and Franklin Roosevelt on economic issues, and both Roosevelts on foreign affairs. In the area of race, with rare exceptions (Truman's decision on armed forces integration was one of these) our presidents—both Republican and Democrat—have chosen to reflect the nation's sentiments rather than steer them.

Events of the Second Reconstruction make clearer than ever that racism is not a sectional characteristic. And in both the North and the South, the tactical requirements for those who believe in racial equality are essentially the same: it is the moral power of aroused people, expressed in protests outside the traditional political channels, that compels a new self-interest for the possessors of power, whether they be in Washington or Atlanta or Birmingham. Nothing so reshuffles the hierarchy of values of a politician—North or South—or gives his dormant conscience a wee breath of life, as a mass demonstration in the streets.

Very close behind racism on that list of traits alleged to be peculiarly Southern is the fact of *violence*. Wilbur J. Cash, in *The Mind of the South*, comes back again and again to this. "I speak of violence. One of the notable results of the spread of the idea of honor, indeed, was an increase in the tendency to violence throughout the social scale." He points to the duel, the "honor complex," and the admiration directed at the man who had slain five or eight or thirteen Negroes. Cash traces the development of the trait from the Old South to the "New South" of industry, commerce, urbanization, and he concludes that despite these changes the old characteristics persist, with violence prominent among them.

Cash dwells on the duel, which we would expect to find in a semi-feudal, manorial society like the Old South. It existed, however, also in the North, throughout our early history; it is identified with the South probably because there it was more frequent and persisted over more generations. The most famous duel in United States history, we might recall, was fought by two New Yorkers, Hamilton and Burr.

When we are dealing with violence as such, however, without regard to its particular forms, the distinction between North and South becomes quite difficult to establish; we cling fondly to traditional notions and dislike testing them. But how can we ignore the West— both North and South, Montana as well as Texas—as the locale of private violence, lawlessness, gun duels, murder? Was Atlanta, Georgia, more violent than Rapid City, South Dakota? It was only the *object* of violence that varied: Indians on the Great Plains, Negroes in the South, Orientals on the West Coast. In the 1880's, while Negroes were being lynched in Mississippi, Chinese were being massacred in Wyoming.

Violence is a national characteristic, not a sectional one. (We could go further, and discuss it as a universal characteristic, but in this argument I am only trying to dispose of the myth of Southern exceptionalism; that of United States exceptionalism would require another book.) Seventeenth-century New Englanders hanged innocent men and women as witches; Puritans killed Indians as savagely as did Virginians. The two important revolts that marked our early history as a nation—Shays' Rebellion and the Whisky Rebellion— took place in the North.

Violence is attached naturally to certain kinds of phenomena, regardless of section. It infects race hatred, which has been greater in the South mainly because there are more Negroes there; it is also a consequence of industrial conflict, which has been more intense in the North, simply because there are more industries there, among other reasons. Thus, the murderous violence of this nation's great labor struggles has taken place mostly outside the South: the railroad riots of 1877 in Baltimore, St. Louis, and points between; the Haymarket bombing in Chicago; the Homestead Strike in Pennsylvania; the Ludlow Massacre in Colorado; the Christmas Day 1913 slaughter in Michigan; the textile strike in Lawrence, Massachusetts; the Memorial Day Massacre in Chicago in the 1930's. Race riots in Northern cities have been as brutal as any riots anywhere. But the myth of a peculiar *Southern* addiction to violence persists.

Cash himself, so fascinated by violence in the South, describes Northern Reconstruction in terms that assault his own thesis: the Yankee, he says, "came back in towering rage and hate, and shorn of all the fine notions of chivalry. . . . Came back to sit down for thirty years this time, to harry the South first with the plan called Thorough and the bayonet. . . . To make the frontier absolute and continual. To rob, to loot, to waste the pitiful remaining substance of this people in riot."

Southern newspapers, with silent malice, respond to Northern reports of race violence in Dixie by playing up crime in New York, Chicago, Philadelphia, Detroit. And of course they are telling the truth, even if they do it as a way of softening their own guilt. Violence is

something to which all human beings everywhere are
prone, whenever other means fail in securing something they desperately want. And unlike other animals,
the human directs his violence not only against immediate obstacles but also against symbols, and thus magnifies thousandfold the potential objects of attack. To
ascribe violence to a particular region or race or social
system relieves us of the necessity of analyzing it as a
human universal.

When Sacco and Vanzetti awaited execution in a
Boston jail, Heywood Broun wrote eloquently and an-
grily about the committee of distinguished Bostonians
who gave their blessing to the sentence, and singled out
especially President Lowell of Harvard. "The tragedy of
it all," Broun wrote, in the *New York World* "lies in
the fact that though a Southern mountain man may
move more quickly to a dirty deed of violence, his feet
are set no more firmly in the path of prejudice than a
Lowell ambling sedately to a hanging." Judicial murder in the form of capital punishment, which is outlawed in only a handful of Northern states, is still predominant as a national policy, and the distinction in
degree between North and South is not as important as
the unity of sections in maintaining a habit which future generations will regard with horror.

Although there is a quantitative difference between
murders in the South and those in the North—both private murders and those indulged in by the state (Georgia happens to be the most murderous)—the essential
sanction to it is given by the nation as a whole, in its literature, its folklore, its laws, its basic dependence on
arms for both internal and external security. It is the
nation's chief law-enforcement officer, J. Edgar Hoover.

who sets the example. In 1960, writing in the FBI *Law Enforcement Bulletin* against those calling for the abolition of capital punishment, he affirmed vigorously the need for a death penalty. (On the other hand, looking farther South than The South, we might note that most Latin American countries have abolished the death penalty.)

The brilliance of William Faulkner and Tennessee Williams has helped perpetuate the belief in a violence peculiar to the South. But we need only to look at Hemingway in the upper literary reaches and Mickey Spillane in the somewhat lower to find violence in our national literature. It is the directness of Hemingway's prose perhaps, that introduces and withdraws cleanly the *motif* of violence; in the Southern writers it hangs in the air, like the smell of the swamp, and affects just a little our capacity to think about it rationally.

None of this is intended to gloss over the particularity of violence, the distinctions in degree or frequency of it among regions of the nation in different times and situations. My aim is only to stop us from using these differences as a way of blocking a gross fact about national character. And if my emphasis right now is on violence as a national trait, rather than as a universal one, it is only because I believe that selectivity in analysis should be geared to possibilities for action. It is in *nations* today that we have the deepest repositories of violence, and it is on a national level that we find at least some access to significant levers of control.

Evangelical religion is another of those qualities we plaster quickly on the South before anyone can notice how strong a strain this has been in the culture of the

United States as a whole. Along with it go fundamentalism, piety, and religiosity in general. True, there
is *more* Baptist emotionalism in the preaching that goes
on in the South, more religious revivalism, more faith
healing, more Bible quoting, more downright religious
hypocrisy. But this is only an intense form of what has
gone on for so long in the whole nation; in the North it
has managed to duck below the level of absurdity just
often enough to steer the chuckles and jibes of the ra-
tionalists toward the harassed South.

If anyone can convince us that there is something
about the South which naturally leads it to religious
primitivism, it is Cash, who writes in *The Mind of the
South* of the Southerner's sense of sin, his fear of
damnation: "The world he knew, the hot sting of the
sun in his blood, the sidelong glance of the all-com-
plaisant Negro woman—all these impelled him irresistibly to joy. But even as he danced, and even though he
had sloughed off all formal religion, his thoughts were
with the piper and his fee."

And it is the physical world of the South, Cash
stresses, that enhances this mood:

> There are days when the booming of the wind
> in the pines is like the audible rushing of time—
> when the sad knowledge of the grave stirs in the
> subconsciousness and bends the spirit to melan-
> choly. . . . And there are those days, too, when
> the earth whimpers in dread, when the lightning
> clicks in awful concatenation with continuous
> thunder, and hurricanes break forth with semi-
> tropical fury; days when this land which, in its
> dominant mood, wraps its children in soft illusion,

> strips them naked before terror. . . . What our Southerner required . . . was a faith as simple and emotional as himself. . . . A faith, not of liturgy and prayer book, but of primitive frenzy and the blood sacrifice. . . .

But Cash is not so carried away that he does not utter the exact truth a paragraph later: "What was demanded here, in other words, was the God and the faith of the Methodists and the Baptists, and the Presbyterians. These personal and often extravagant sects, sweeping the entire American country with their revivals in the first half of the nineteenth century, achieved their greatest success in the personal and extravagant South" The South, Cash tells us here clearly, saw sectarian, primitive religion at its most intense. But the phenomenon itself was a national one. Both statements are true. The second one, however, has been glossed over in the fond romanticization of the South as an area apart from the rest.

And was it only in the South that the forest pressed close, its darkness spawning wild thoughts in the brain? "The edge of the wilderness was close by. The American continent stretched endlessly west, and it was full of mystery for them. It stood, dark and threatening over their shoulders night and day, for out of it Indian tribes marauded from time to time. . . ." This is Arthur Miller's description of seventeenth-century Salem, Massachusetts, in *The Crucible*.

New England was the birthplace of revivalism, through the voice of Jonathan Edwards. In 1741 when he delivered his masterpiece in Enfield, Massachusetts, "Sinner in the Hands of An Angry God," his listeners moaned, shrieked, cried out, until he had to pause. It was the beginning of The Great Awakening, and it soon got out of hand. Perry Miller wrote in *Jonathan Edwards:* "The land was filled with enthusiasm, not just the faintings of 1740, and orgies too fantastic to be credible mounted, while the bastardy rate began to rise."

Shortly after the American Revolution, revivalist religion seems to have sprung up North and South, and especially along the Western frontier of both sections. When the wall of a church collapsed at Jones' Hole, Virginia, in 1787, in the midst of a revival, the frenzied dancing and shouting continued through the rain of bricks until everyone was exhausted. Violent religious meetings spread through Kentucky and Tennessee in the early nineteenth century. Twenty thousand people attended one five-day camp meeting in Kentucky. An observer wrote: "Some of the people were singing, others praying, some crying for mercy in the most piteous accents, while others were shouting most vociferously. . . . At one time I saw at least five hundred swept down in a moment, as if a battery of a thousand guns had been opened upon them, and then immediately followed shrieks and shouts that rent the very heavens."

These scenes were easily matched in Western New York in the 1820's, where Charles G. Finney started on a rampage of revival meetings that carried him into major cities of the East and Midwest. The religious excitement at those meetings reached points of frenzy induced by Finney's verbal pictures of the terror of hell. It was The Great Revival, and it spread, North and South and West into the antebellum period. The ones held on Long Island perhaps never matched those held in Georgia, one of which is described by Alice Felt Tyler in *Freedom's Ferment:* "The grandeur of the night meeting in the forest, the eight fine altars, the campfires of resinous wood, the superb singing of the thousands of Negroes, the wails of the penitent, the thunder and lightning of an approaching storm. . . ." But despite differences in tone and style, the camp meeting, and the religious primitivism it represented, were national phenomena.

Dwight Moody, the colorful evangelist of the late nineteenth century, was from Massachusetts. Although he stressed love and mercy rather than hell-fire and damnation, his approach was a fundamentalist one. The Bible Institute he established remains in Chicago. Around the same time, the Jehovah's Witnesses group originated with the followers of Charles Russell, a Pennsylvanian who did much of his work in New York City and who preached a fundamentalism as stark as anything seen in the South. We might note too that, although Tennessee gave us the famous *Scopes Case* by passing a law that barred evolutionist teaching which contradicted the Bible, the man who acted as chief witness for the Tennessee Bible crowd was William Jennings Bryan, son of the Midwest. Evangelist Billy Sunday was also a Midwesterner. Historically, fundamentalism is ingrained in the religious tradition of the entire nation, and it leads to a perpetual tension over the constitutional requirement that church and state be separated.

The fact that the social gospel idea, which attracted a tiny part of the American clergy in the early twentieth century, existed mostly in the North, has been used to create an illusion of religious progressiveness in the North and conservatism in the South. More accurate is the statement that religion throughout the nation has been a conservative force with no more than a few voices, anywhere, trying to be heard above the pious din. The geographic location of the social gospelers has shifted, depending on where there was a rising movement of general social protest, for the church latched onto going movements more often than it started its own. It was the Progressive swell of the turn of the century, concentrated in the North, that encouraged the rise of the social gospel idea there. The second coming of the social gospel has been in the South, in our own era, represented by the Martin Luther Kings, the Ralph Abernathys, and other militants of the Negro churches.

Stow Persons, in his *American Minds,* notes how little real hold the social gospel movement took in the religious life of the nation, despite bursts of fervor and the momentary attention that the outcries of protest received. "In no denomination did the group of social-gospel advocates constitute more than a small minority, albeit a vocal one." He points out that the social gospelers "were more than balanced by fundamentalist wings that continued to stress the old individualistic evangelical piety. By mid-twentieth century, it was apparent that no denomination had in any substantial way been transformed by the social gospel."

There is an undeniable reality about the Bible Belt which stretches through the South. But it does not end there. It winds into the Midwest, and touches every corner of the nation, though not as solidly, or as confidently, as in the South. The placing of Bibles in hotel rooms is a national practice, and there are no indications that the Gideon Society favors any one section. Although the Bible undoubtedly plays an obtrusive role in the public education of the South, most of the Supreme Court cases involving the use of public facilities for religious education have originated in Northern communities.

Jesus lived and died well before the rise of modern nations, and God presumably is not only international, but interplanetary, hardly noticing from his distant post those peculiar boundaries which on our earth mark off nations. But the churches of the United States are national and nationalist. This has been even more true of churches in other nations (the Roman Catholic Church in Italy, the Protestant churches under Hitler, the Russian Orthodox Church, the Church of England), and I mention this because if I am claiming religiosity as a national characteristic, I should note that there is a reverberation between church and nation which often makes the former more national and the latter more pious.

Our society, Max Lerner says in *America As a Civilization,* is a striking mixture of religion and secularism, but he goes on to say what a strong hold religion has on the American character. There is "less and less room for the 'godless' in America, since godlessness is usually associated with Communism and depravity." We are a "Christian country" and, Lerner says: "There is no candidate for even minor political office in America today who would dare to mock religion or alienate any of the denominations. In every major speech a President is likely to include what Franklin Roosevelt used to call the 'God stuff'." And indeed, the speeches of Eisenhower and Kennedy were heavily sprinkled with references to God. The separation of church and state in America is largely a theoretical postulate.

Xenophobia is widespread in the South, as anyone who moves into the region, or travels through it, soon recognizes. It is one of the curious paradoxes of Southern life that suspicion of strangers, of outsiders, goes along with what is called "Southern hospitality." The answer to the paradox is that there is a line of demarcation which separates the accepted person from the unaccepted. Within that line, the warmth is almost overwhelming. But outside it, the coolness can become hostility to the point of violence. The foreign-born is almost always outside that line in the South, as is, of course, the Negro. So Southern hospitality exists, but within rigidly defined limits.

But isn't this true, though to a lesser extent, of the nation? Americans are considered generally to be warm and friendly people, unlike, let us say, the English. If other peoples criticize us, it is rather for being overbearingly friendly rather than withdrawn. We welcomed, let us recall, tens of millions of people from other countries to our shores, with virtually no restriction, for most of our history. But we too laid down our lines, and once laid down, those outside them were treated as coldly, as suspiciously, as any Yankee traveler in the Southern hills.

We began in 1882, with the Chinese, whom we had eagerly sought right after the Civil War as cheap labor to work on the railroads and in the mines, but who later were wanted neither by the industrialists nor the labor unions. The result was the Chinese Exclusion Act of that year. That inaugurated a period of seventy years during which we said very plainly to Asians, in the stiff words of a legislative enactment, that we wanted none of their kind in this country. Our national attitude toward Orientals was one reason for increasing irritation in our relations with Japan all through the early twentieth century up to Pearl Harbor. And our policy toward the immigration of Orientals today, as expressed in the McCarran-Walter Act of 1952, is hardly more friendly: we will admit a hundred Japanese a year, a hundred Chinese, a hundred Indonesians, as compared to tens of thousands for each major country in Western Europe. The message reads clearly to them: in the United States Asians are not wanted.

Our quotas are higher for Europeans, but still there are quotas. Nativism as a private action goes back to the early nineteenth-century resentment of the Irish immigrant; as a public policy it was first written into law in the 1920's, and it remains on our national statute books in the quota system of the McCarran-Walter Act. The line remains drawn against foreigners, though the placement of the line varies, depending on where the stranger comes from. Hospitality—in the law—goes first to the English, Irish, and Germans. The Italians, Greeks, and Eastern Europeans are definitely second-hand recipients of welcome. Africans and Asians are last.

Oscar Handlin's sympathetic study of immigrants, *The Uprooted,* which won a Pulitzer Prize, represents the more enlightened thinking in America on the subject of the foreign-born. But more Americans, I suspect, have gone along with the attitude of another historian, Samuel Orth, who wrote a study of immigrants called *Our Foreigners.* Orth saw the people of the Revolutionary epoch—Scotch, English, Irish, German, Dutch—as the "basic American stock." He then said:

> Leadership . . . is the gift of but few races; and in the U.S. eminence in business, in statecraft, in letters and learning can with singular directness be traced in a preponderating proportion to this American stock. . . . The Puritan, Cavalier, Quaker, Scotch-Irish, Huguenot, and Dutch pioneers were not ordinary folk in any sense of the term. They were, in a measure, a race of heroes. Their sons and grandsons inherited their vigor and their striving. It is not at all singular that every president of the United States and every chief justice of the Federal Supreme Court has come from this stock. . . .

Orth's views were set down in the early part of this century, but public-opinion polls of recent years indicate that the population is not much different today. A 1950 study by Hyman and Sheatsley concluded: "The majority of Americans appear to deny still another traditional feature of democracy, that of offering political asylum and refuge to homeless and oppressed peoples. Faced with the simple proposition of whether or not to admit a certain number of displaced persons from Europe, less than one person in four approved."

The same study found that most Americans who were given a list of seventeen nationalities found only five of these "as good as we are in all important respects." These were: the Canadians, English, Dutch, Scandinavians, and Irish. The rest were judged "not quite as good" or "definitely inferior."

Nativism not only keeps people out: it affects our

relationship with those who have come in. And from the Alien Acts of 1798 to the Alien Registration Act of 1940 and the McCarran-Walter Act of 1952, our national policy has been to look with suspicion on the non-citizen.

Aliens must register every year with the government. An alien, in American judicial doctrine, is not entitled to the same constitutional rights accorded a citizen. An alien, for instance, can be deported for an act which has been made a crime *ex post facto,* though the Constitution bars *ex post facto* laws to punish Americans. Because aliens are tied in with foreign policy, an area where the national government has almost unlimited powers, Congress has broad legislative authority over them to an extent not true of citizens.

Even a person who has already become a citizen through naturalization is not looked upon by our government as an equal with all other United States citizens. According to the McCarran-Walter Act of 1952, if a naturalized citizen is convicted of contempt of Congress for refusing, within ten years of his naturalization, to testify before a congressional committee on his "subversive" activities, he may be deported. In other words, the Fifth Amendment provision against self-incrimination, and the First Amendment (which in some cases protects against political interrogation), cannot protect the naturalized citizen in any event, so long as the law remains what it is.

Until our national policies—on immigration, on aliens, on naturalization—are changed, until our national attitudes get closer to our oratorical claims, it ill becomes us to let the South bear the burden of the charge of nativism or xenophobia.

• • •

The deification of Southern womanhood, more a subject for bemused wonder than for intellectual analysis, has brought both admiration and ridicule. Cash calls it "downright gyneolatry." He says:

> She was the South's Palladium, this Southern woman—the shield-bearing Athena gleaming whitely in the clouds, the standard for its rallying, the mystic symbol of its nationality in face of the foe. She was the lily-pure maid of Astolat and the hunting goddess of the Boeotian hill. And—she was the pitiful Mother of God. Merely to mention her was to send strong men into tears—or shouts. There was hardly a sermon that did not begin and end with tributes in her honor, hardly a brave speech that did not open and close with the clashing of shields and the flourishing of swords for her glory. At the last, I verily believe, the ranks of the Confederacy went rolling into battle in the misty conviction that it was wholly for her that they fought.

When Georgia celebrated her 100th anniversary in the 1830's, the toast was cheered twenty times: "Woman! The center and circumference, diameter and periphery, sine, tangent, and secant of all our affections!" And into the twentieth century the basic romantic myth remains the same: in the South the woman is ennobled and glorious—only Robert E. Lee stands higher on his pedestal than she does.

Once the florid oratory is set aside, however, the elevation of woman—at least as a surface phenomenon—is seen to be a fact of national life. Tocqueville watched it in the North in the 1830's, and travelers from Europe and the Far East in this century show wonder at the degree of equality between men and women. The growing role of the President's wife, transformed from social accessory to thinking companion, is symbolic of what has been happening in this country: as total personalities, Eleanor Roosevelt and Jacqueline Kennedy were unmatched by presidents' wives of earlier centuries.

And then there is Marilyn Monroe. Deification moves from metaphor to reality with her, for she was a goddess to the American public, and her death was received as an almost religious mystery. Hollywood has supplied the nation with feminine objects of worship in a continuous stream, from Mary Pickford through Jean Harlow, Greta Garbo, Ingrid Bergman, and the wide-eyed Marilyn.

But now that we've paid obeisance to the tradition of glorification, we need to bring the analysis somewhat closer to the truth, both for the South and the nation. There were several crucial limitations to the Southern attitude. Remember, the phrase is really "Southern *white* womanhood." And *rich* white womanhood, too —for the poor white wife was hardly an object of worship in the South, then or now. The miserable, overworked Southern white woman, bred in poverty, who spends much of her time in labor bearing children, and the rest of her time in labor between childbirths, is a thousand times more numerous than Scarlett O'Hara.

And even the white aristocratic woman, back in slavery days—how genuine was the veneration, how deep the reverence, when the man of the house rushed as often as he could into sexual union with brown and black women? The existence of millions of tan and fair

Negroes in America belies the image of the glorified Southern white woman. What more damning reminder is there of the emptiness of that claim that the white woman was the "center and circumference . . ." of affection than the fact that so often she waited at the periphery while her man was having sexual relations with a darker woman? The hurtful fact about the woman on the pedestal is that she is quite alone.

For the nation, as for the South, the fuss about womanhood has always been somewhat dishonest. The Southern veneration was circumscribed with modifications—whiteness, aristocratic birth, wealth, idleness; so was this true in the United States as a whole. In the country at large, to be considered superior a woman must have certain qualifications: beauty or talent, foremost. Brains alone, however, are not enough for a woman to gain genuine recognition. Mental agility, superior intelligence, bring tolerance and respect, but nothing like idolization; that is reserved for Venus or Diana, not for the lady Ph.D.

The difference in accent, North and South, the soft consonants and prolonged vowels of the Southern woman, conceal the essential similarity of the position of women in the nation, regardless of geographic section. The haughty Daughter of the Confederacy with the big hat at the garden club in Charleston, South Carolina, can hardly be distinguished, except in speech, from the equally haughty, equally big-hatted Daughter of the American Revolution at a lawn party in Newport, Rhode Island. Women in the textile mills, North and South, wear the same slacks, the same bandannas, and the same look of alienation from life.

Cash speaks of the "suppression of class feeling" in the South, both before the Civil War and after Reconstruction. He attributes this "social solidity" to the existence of the Negro as a drain for the ego of the Southern white, drawing off what might have been a natural hostility to the rich, Southern white man. And true, it was only *before* the cotton gin magnified and solidified slavery in the nineteenth century that occasional violent class explosions shook the South.

Bacon's Rebellion of 1676 was only one of many signs of sharp hostility between the frontier farmers and the seaboard aristocracy in Virginia and Maryland. And a century later, the Regulator Movement in the Carolinas expressed, by force of arms, resentments of the poor against the wealthy. In that hundred years between, many clashes of a class nature took place in the Southern colonies. What was said by a contemporary of Bacon was true of much of the South during that period: "Indigent People as had no benefits from the Taxes groaned under our being thus overborn."

No doubt the Negro, as slave before the Civil War and as semi-slave after the War, formed some sort of a block between the downtrodden white and the Southern aristocracy and diverted attention from obvious differences in wealth. Up North, in the same years when Nat Turner's insurrection was fresh in Virginia minds, workingmen were organizing in the cities of New York and Philadelphia. And the year 1877, which for the South meant preoccupation with the restoration of white supremacy, was the year when gunfire sounded along the railroad lines of the Northeast, and railway workers fought bloody battles against employers over wages and working conditions.

I am trying, in these paragraphs, to do justice to the real difference between North and South in the matter of class conflict and class consciousness, before I move to what I think is the larger truth and the more significant one for our national history: that such differences between North and South have been matters of degree, based on time and circumstance. In the longer perspective, both sections—Americans as a whole—despite periods of sporadic conflict, have moved into a semi-happy narcosis in which consciousness of class has been dulled.

That the South is perfectly capable of *class* violence is shown by the revolts referred to above in the colonial period and by isolated situations, like the Gastonia textile strike of the 1920's, as bitter in its own way as was the Lawrence, Massachusetts, textile strike of a decade earlier. That the South is also capable of subordinating race to class is shown in that brief interlude of the Populist period in the South, when there was some evidence that white and black farmers could be drawn together by common grievances against "the interests." And we get a glimmer of the possible in the South's embrace of Franklin D. Roosevelt during the depression.

True, the North between 1877 and 1940 (such a short span in our history, really!) was the scene of our most intense labor struggles, but this can be laid to the circumstances that brought industrial growth to that area first. And it is in the first agony of such growth (almost as peasants revolted against the Soviet collectivization of the thirties before settling down to live with it) that rebellion occurs. But there is nothing in "the Southern mind," no mystical quality of the Southern temper, which prevents the Southerner from feeling class hostility. As racism erodes and industrialization develops in the South, that chance may come.

True, our national class grievances are nowhere near as sharp as they might be; the distribution of wealth in Latin America, in the Middle East, is unspeakably more uneven. Yet we do have our poor. A substantial part of the nation has to battle every day to keep the family fed, clothed, sheltered, and alive. But the hurt is not so keen, apparently, that it cannot be suppressed by an injection of nationalism; this has always been the salve for internal discomfort, and it has never been available in such gross quantities as now.

Nationalism, manifested extremely in patriotism and super-patriotism, has often been seen as a distinctive Southern trait—oddly juxtaposed with the South's own jealous sectionalism. Aside from those few years around the Civil War, the South has been recognized as the most jingoistic of the sections, the most loudly reverent of country, flag, national honor. After all, the Daughters of the American Revolution go further back than the Daughters of the Confederacy, and are especially strong in the South. A formidable quintet of Virginians—Washington, Jefferson, Madison, Monroe, John Marshall—founded our nation and dominated those early patriotic years.

Southern estrangement from the nation during the Civil War soon ended, and when we fought Spanish armies in Cuba, the Gray stood alongside the Blue. After Appomattox, as before Bull Run, Southern men were especially prominent in the national military establishment. So the emphasis has continued to this day on the idea of a particularly "militant South."

And it is true. Yet, to dwell on that obscures another truth, perhaps more necessary to sober us in today's world; that militant nationalism has been a persistent United States tradition.

Today, sprawled comfortably across the continent from ocean to ocean, our eyes on the galaxies, we are bemused and irritated at what seems a petulant nationalism in the new nations of Africa and Asia. But we were quite feverish in those first decades after the Revolution—eyeing Canada and Florida, snapping at England, France, and Spain, finally devouring half of Mexico in a burst of indignation. Tocqueville had written, in Jackson's time: "Nothing is more embarrassing in the ordinary intercourse of life than this irritable patriotism of the Americans."

Still, nationalism was contained within the continent through most of the nineteenth century; we left Europe and Asia alone. Even after the Spanish-American War, perhaps because we were full of moralistic protestations, perhaps because the European powers were dividing up the world, we still had a look of innocence. This was not easy to maintain, because now we were firmly planted, not only in the Caribbean, but on the other side of the Pacific Ocean.

When we did enter European affairs in World Wars I and II, it was with grand pronouncements. We fought to make the world safe for democracy the first time, to save the world from Hitlerism the second time; the idea that national interest—imagined in the first instance and real in the second—lay behind it all, was kept obscure. The sixteen billion dollars we gave through the Marshall Plan after the war was seen, not as a power move sweetened with good intention, but as nothing more than a sincere effort on our part to help the fallen

world. That Asia, Africa, and Eastern Europe were more
fallen but less politically susceptible was overlooked.

In the 1960's, if it was not clear before, it is now:
Americans as a whole are hot for patriotism, armed and
challenging and as self-glorifying as any Southern orator ever was.

Edmund Wilson, in *Patriotic Gore,* points out that
the South, in the Civil War, always had its "Great
Alibi" for retrogression and that the North has had its
"Treasury of Virtue," which "has enabled us to carry
along into all our subsequent wars . . . the insuffer-
able moral attitudes that appeared to us first to be
justified by our victory over the Confederacy in 1865."

The same goes for conservatism. It was the South
that always talked of defending its "way of life." The
nation was young, vigorous, forward-looking, the leg-
end goes, and the South was recalcitrant, hugging its
traditions, fearful of progress. Supporting this is the fact
of our revolutionary tradition. Did not Tocqueville
have to explain our rash radicalism, our equalitarianism, our upstart ideas, to the conservatives of Metter-
nichean Europe? The reality of that revolutionary
spirit is gone, but its aura remains, with which we find it
convenient to belabor the "conservative South."

Today, however, it is the United States that talks of
defending "its way of life" against revolutionary threats
all over the world. We are now the conservative nation,
trying to maintain the status quo against what appears to
be a torrent of change threatening Western civilization.
I am not attempting to assess the quality of our revolutionary ideals of the past as against the quality of
the present upsurge, but only to assert that we stand

fast, guarding the present, with as much nervous fear
as any Southern politician has who holds on to what he is
sure of, against the uncertainties of transformation.

The South is poor. Franklin D. Roosevelt called it
the "Number One economic problem" of the United
States. In 1959, when the median income for the
United States was $5,600, in Mississippi it was $2,800,
exactly half. While in that year thirteen per cent of the
nation's families earned under $2,000, the percentage
for Alabama was 26 per cent, for Georgia 22 per cent,
for Mississippi 37 per cent. Poverty marks the South today as clearly as cotton once did.

I do not want to challenge the fact that the South is
poorer than the rest of the nation. But I do want to
point to something which has been often overlooked
(though in the year 1963, notice began to be taken):
that there are large and numerous pockets of poverty
in the United States as shocking as that one which is the
South; that the idea of a rich North and a poor South is
demolished by the statistics and the stories of human
despair which come out of the cities of the North, out
of the rundown little towns of New England and the
Midwest. The divisions of rich and poor in this country
do not run along sectional lines but exist, to different
degrees, in every section of the country.

We reject poverty as a national problem when we
relegate it to the South, with the implication that this
is a startling divergence from the general United States
picture of prosperity. A more accurate image is of a
land where thin threads of wealth run through all the
sections, along with broad shaded areas representing
middle-class, mortgaged affluence, and of millions of

people *everywhere,* fighting to meet the basic requirements of life for themselves and their children.

The realities of life are obscured under meaningless statistics when we measure the wealth of people in huge aggregates, pushing all people into one section or taking a national average. To say that the national average income is $5,600 is impressive in giving a picture of a quite well-off nation, but it doesn't do justice to the distinctions by group. When we move slightly closer to piecemeal examination, more light is shed on the subject of income distribution: in 1960, the lowest fifth of the United States population averaged about $1,500 a year in income and the highest fifth averaged about $15,000. And this is only the beginning of the process of making distinctions within the national average, only the first step toward a truly human appraisal of the extent of poverty in the United States. The details themselves have been well told in Michael Harrington's *The Other America* and Leon Keyserling's *Poverty and Deprivation in the U.S.*

Let me go back over my argument. The South is everything its revilers have charged, and more than its defenders have claimed. It is racist, violent, hypocritically pious, xenophobic, false in its elevation of women, nationalistic, conservative, and it harbors extreme poverty in the midst of ostentatious wealth. The only point I have to add is that the United States, as a civilization, embodies all of those same qualities. That the South possesses them with more intensity simply makes it easier for the nation to pass off its characteristics to the South, leaving itself innocent and righteous.

In any truth which is knotted and complex, we can choose what strand we want to grasp. To pick out the South has the advantage of focusing attention on what is worst; but it has the disadvantage of glossing over the faults of the nation. It is particularly appropriate in this time, when the power of the United States gives it enormous responsibility, to focus our critical faculties on those qualities which mark—or disfigure—our nation. With this approach, the South becomes not damnable, but marvelously useful, as a mirror in which the nation can see its blemishes magnified, so that it will hurry to correct them. In effective psychotherapy, the patient is at first disturbed by self-recognition, then grateful for the disclosure. It is the first step toward transformation, and in the 1960's, this nation, with its huge potential for good, needs to take another look in the mirror. We owe this to ourselves, and to our children.

Bibliographical Notes

Sɪɴᴄᴇ this book is primarily a speculative essay based on personal experience, I have not drawn up a formal bibliography. Nevertheless, I do want to call attention to certain books and articles that have stimulated my thinking, provided supporting facts, or otherwise had an effect on what has gone into this book.

In Part One, "Is the Southern White Unfathomable?" what started as a germ of an idea based on observation and experience became strengthened as I began to read the literature of post-Freudian psychology and certain works of sociology and history. Stanley Elkins's *Slavery* (University of Chicago Press, 1959), besides providing provocative insights, helped me to find a direction for my own thoughts. In one of the classics of sociological literature, E. A. Ross's *Social Control* (Macmillan, 1901), I found a perceptive set of distinctions relating to the attitudes of people involved in social change, and a very useful discussion of the relative weights of moral sentiment and self-interest in activating people. Another sociologist of the same generation, Charles H. Cooley, in *Social Organization* (Scribner's, 1909), made some interesting observations on conformity and its social uses. Karl Mannheim's *Ideology and Utopia* (Harcourt, Brace, 1940), is rich in comments on the participating intellectual, and the possibility of the social scientist being both a scholar and an activist. Robert K. Merton's *Social*

Theory and Social Structure (Free Press, 1949) strengthened the conviction that the accuracy of social analysis depends on *social controls.* Melvin Tumin, in *Desegregation: Resistance and Readiness* (Princeton University Press, 1958), gives solid support, it seems to me, to the importance of distinguishing between idea and *action* in the attitudes and behavior of white Southerners. Sociologist Arnold M. Rose, in his article "The Influence of Legislation on Prejudice" in *Common Ground* (1949), showed early the value of firm authority in changing social practices. Among the social psychologists, there is, first, Harry Stack Sullivan, who, in *The Interpersonal Theory of Psychiatry* (Norton, 1953), buttresses optimism about the capacity of the white Southerner (and the white Northerner) to change his behavior swiftly. Kurt Lewin, in *Field Theory in Social Science* (Harper, 1951), goes into great detail to describe the effects of the *present* field on human behavior. Dorwin Cartwright continued Lewin's experimentation, and reports on some of this in his article "Achieving Change in People," *Human Relations* (1951). I found particularly stimulating Gardner Murphy's *Personality,* and its discussion of "situationism" and "role." A good survey of the whole subject is in J. A. C. Brown's *Freud and the Post-Freudians* (Penguin Books, 1961). In Herbert Marcuse's *Eros and Civilization* (Beacon Press, 1955) and Norman O. Brown's *Life Against Death* (Wesleyan University Press, 1959), we have two brilliant arguments against what Marcuse calls "neo-Freudian revisionism." The social psychologist who has applied "situationist" theories most closely to the present race problem in America is Thomas Pettigrew, as in his article "Social Psychology and Desegregation Research," in *American Psychologist* (1961). A strong influence along the same lines is Gordon Allport, *The Nature of Prejudice* (Beacon Press, 1954). For a fresh view of race relations in the post-bellum South, I drew upon C. Vann Woodward, *The Strange Career of Jim Crow* (Oxford University Press, 1957). Also a new Southern view is that of Dewey Grantham, *The Democratic South* (University of Georgia Press, 1963).

Part Two, "The 'Mysterious' Negro," is even more of a personal commentary than the first part of the book, and so does not come, at least directly, from other published works. Perhaps the best single dispeller of mystique about the Negro is W. E. B. DuBois's beautiful book, *Souls of Black Folk* (A. C. McClung, 1922). And I found many keen observations about Negro society today in E. Franklin Frazier's *Black Bourgeoisie* (Free Press, 1959). I was spurred to think about causation by reading in the philosophy of history, and found some support in E. H. Carr's *What Is History?* (Knopf, 1962), which advances something like the idea of "operable" cause which I set forth in this section.

Part Three, "Albany, Georgia: Ghost in the Cage," is based on personal experience and observation, interviews, and the newspaper reports during the Albany, Georgia, crises of 1961 and 1962, collected while I was doing my reports for the Southern Regional Council in Atlanta. The legal argumentation in this chapter utilizes material from the volume *Justice* put out in 1961 by the U. S. Commission on Civil Rights. I found Jack Greenberg's *Race Relations and American Law* (Columbia University Press, 1959) an indispensable reference work.

In Part Four, "The South as a Mirror," my starting point was Wilbur J. Cash's *The Mind of the South* (Knopf, 1946), a beautifully written book which captures so much of the South, past and present, and yet which also may have a narcotic effect on one's will for change. For the early history of the Negro in America, I have depended on John Hope Franklin, *From Slavery to Freedom* (Knopf, 1956). Valuable for the nineteenth century is Fanny Kemble's *Journal* (Carey, Lea, and Blanchard, 1835). Some of the material on abolitionism and on revivalism is drawn from Alice Felt Tyler's *Freedom's Ferment* (University of Minnesota, 1944). The reference to Richard Hofstadter's comment on the Emancipation Proclamation comes from one of the great books written by this generation of historians, his *The American Political Tradition* (Knopf, 1948). Material on anti-Negro attitudes in Michigan during Reconstruction came from an unpublished work by Ida Meltzer, *The Negro in Michigan 1865-70*. The brief comments on the social gospel movement are based on Stow Persons's *American Minds* (Holt, 1958).

About the Author

Howard Zinn is professor emeritus at Boston University. He is the author of the classic *A People's History of the United States,* "a brilliant and moving history of the American people from the point of view of those . . . whose plight has been largely omitted from most histories" *(Library Journal).* Zinn has received the Lannan Foundation Literary Award for Nonfiction and the Eugene V. Debs award for his writing and political activism. He is the author of numerous books, including *The Zinn Reader,* the autobiographical *You Can't Be Neutral on a Moving Train,* and the plays *Marx in Soho* (South End Press) and *Emma* (South End Press).

Zinn grew up in Brooklyn and worked in the shipyards before serving as an Air Force bombardier in World War II. Zinn was chair of the History Department at Spelman College, where he actively participated in the civil rights movement, before taking a position at Boston University. He now lives with his wife, Roslyn, in Massachusetts and lectures widely on history and contemporary politics.

Seven of Zinn's books have been republished by South End Press as part of its new Radical Sixties series, which seeks to make available new editions of essential works that relate to or are inspired by the political struggles of the 1960s.

Books by Howard Zinn

Emma. Cambridge: South End Press, 2002.
Terrorism and War. New York: Seven Stories Press, 2002.
Howard Zinn on War. New York: Seven Stories Press, 2001.
Howard Zinn on History. New York: Seven Stories Press, 2001.
Marx in Soho: A Play on History. Cambridge: South End Press, 1999.
The Future of History: Interviews with David Barsamian. Monroe, Maine: Common Courage Press, 1999.
A People's History of the United States: 1492–Present, Twentieth Anniversary Edition. New York: HarperCollins, 1999.
The Zinn Reader: Writings on Disobedience and Democracy. New York: Seven Stories Press, 1997.
You Can't Be Neutral on a Moving Train: A Personal History of Our Times. Boston: Beacon Press, 1994.
Declarations of Independence: Cross-Examining American Ideology. New York: HarperCollins, 1990.
The Politics of History, 2nd ed. Urbana: University of Illinois Press, 1990.

See also the other six volumes by Howard Zinn in the South End Press Radical Sixties series.

The Radical Sixties Series

The Southern Mystique is volume 2 in South End Press's new Radical Sixties series, which seeks to make available new editions of essential works that relate to or are inspired by the political struggles of the 1960s. Other titles in the series are:

Volume 1
SNCC: The New Abolitionists
by Howard Zinn
ISBN 0-89608-679-8
$15.00

Volume 3
Vietnam: The Logic of Withdrawal
by Howard Zinn
ISBN 0-89608-681-X
$15.00

Volume 4
Disobedience and Democracy: Nine Fallacies of Law and Order
by Howard Zinn
ISBN 0-89608-675-5
$15.00

Volume 5
Postwar America: 1945–1971
by Howard Zinn
ISBN 0-89608-678-X
$15.00

Volume 6
Justice in Everyday Life: The Way It Really Works
by Howard Zinn
ISBN 0-89608-677-1
$15.00

Volume 7
Failure to Quit: Reflections of an Optimistic Historian
by Howard Zinn
ISBN 0-89608-676-3
$15.00

Volume 8
Prelude to Revolution: France in May 1968
Second Edition
by Daniel Singer
ISBN 0-89608-676-3
$15.00

About South End Press

South End Press is a nonprofit, collectively run book publisher with more than 200 titles in print. Since our founding in 1977, we have tried to meet the needs of readers who are exploring, or are already committed to, the politics of radical social change.

Our goal is to publish books that encourage critical thinking and constructive action on the key political, cultural, social, economic, and ecological issues shaping life in the United States and in the world. In this way, we hope to give expression to a wide diversity of democratic social movements and to provide an alternative to the products of corporate publishing.

To order books, please send a check or money order to: South End Press, 7 Brookline Street, #1, Cambridge, MA 02139-4146. Or call 1-800-533-8478. Please include $3.50 for postage and handling for the first book and 50 cents for each additional book. Write or e-mail us at southend@southendpress.org for a free catalog, or visit our website at http://www.southendpress.org.